Author Biography

I was born in London, England and immigrated to Canada with my parents when I was seventeen. I attended Trinity College at the University of Toronto, and emerged with a degree in French and English. I became a secretary for a large corporation and met my future husband, Ed, not long after that. In 1980, we moved to Alberta, where he set up a chiropractic office, and we raised a family in Okotoks. Inspired by our daughter, Amy, we got involved in amateur theatre and still pursue it as a hobby. I have worked in many administrative jobs, but have always wanted to write. We continue to live in Okotoks, and enjoy theatre, music and travel.

Debbie Sands , 2015

Thank you so much for you support!
Debbie

A Moth to the Flame
The story of Amy's struggle with borderline personality disorder

by Debbie Sands

Second printing February 2017.

Sands, Debbie (1952-)

ISBN-13: 978-0-9686646-7-4 (Crossfield Publishing)

Cataloguing in Publication Data

Non-Fiction, biography, psychology

1. psychology/mental illness 2. borderline personality disorder 3. BPD 4. mentally ill/biography 5. mental illness/case studies 6. mentally ill children/biography 7. dialectical behavior therapy 8. DBT 9. children/ justice system

Cover artwork by Lawrence Stilwell

Interior layout by Harald Kunze

Manuscript prepared by Crossfield Publishing

Editing and Foreward by Fran L. Porter, author of *When the Ship Has No Stabilizers: our daughter's tempestuous voyage through borderline personality disorder*, 2014.

Crossfield Publishing   www.crossfieldpublishing.ca   1-226-301-4001

2269 Road 120, R7, St. Marys, Ontario, N4X 1C9, Canada

All the photographs in this book are from the Sands family albums except for the last image on pg. 146 and the lake at Kelowna, BC, which is from "Mark's" collection, pg. 99.

Reviewer's reference: A.E. Jongsma, L. M. Peterson, W. P. McInnis, 2011. *Adult, Adolescent & Child Psychotherapy Treatment Planners*, Hoboken, NJ: John Wiley & Sons Inc.

Printed in Canada by Houghton Boston, Saskatoon, SK

CROSSFIELD
PUBLISHING

Acknowledgements

Many people have inspired me to write this book – it started when Amy was a teenager, and I told many of my friends who were in shock when I described her behaviour and run-ins with the law that I was going to write a book about her some day. They all told me that I should but, at that time, I never really thought I would. I assumed that she would grow up and one day leave behind her difficult behaviour and criminal associations and become a normal, mature adult.

After we lost her, our lives were turned upside down and, other than speaking about her to various groups and parents with difficult children, the thought of a book still didn't re-surface. Then we met Fran Porter. She had lost her daughter to Borderline Personality Disorder, although under different circumstances, and had successfully written a book about their experiences with her ("When the Ship has no Stabilizers", Fran L. Porter, Crossfield Publishing, 2014). My husband, Ed, and I immediately bonded with Fran on our first meeting and recognized so many similarities in our two daughters. I told her that I wanted to write about Amy, and both she and her husband, Andy, encouraged me to do so. In fact, Fran very kindly edited the grammar and syntax for me on many occasions! Thank you, Fran – without your support, I never would have been able to put pen to paper.

Secondly, my publisher, Tina Crossfield. Thank you for your words of wisdom and unwavering support. I first told Tina at Fran's book launch that I wanted to write about Amy, and she reminded me that I knew "where to find her". That thought encouraged me to sit down and start writing not long afterwards. For all of your help, support, suggestions and patience – thank you, Tina!

Many thanks to Larry Stilwell, for stepping up to create a beautiful artwork for the front cover based on a "very small" photo reference, as well as designing the book's front and back covers. Your talent is exceptional.

To all of my friends who also encouraged me – Sue, Florence, Michele, Nicola, Tracy, Colleen and Jim – while I was still going through the writing process, thank you! To those who urged me to see it through – Linda, Deb, Kevin, my mother Valerie, my co-workers, thank you.

There are many others whom I have not named, but please know that I value your support.

Actual names have been changed to protect identities, other than when permission was granted.

To my children, Stephanie and Michael, who accompanied us on the journey with Amy, thank you for your love and patience! Thank you for your understanding, for allowing us to focus on Amy's problems when you often must have felt that you were deserving of the same attention, and for taking this voyage of grief and loss with us. We love you, and take great comfort in your presence in our lives.

And last of all, but never least, thank you to my husband, Ed. You suffered Amy's terrible loss with me as a parent and were always my greatest support. You helped and encouraged me with this book, and often corrected a timeline, or provided a better way of saying something. Without you, the book would never have happened, and it has certainly been a healing journey for us both. Thank you for everything.

Dedication

*To the memory of our beautiful daughter Amy, and to my family, Ed,
Stephanie, Michael and Luc, who travelled this journey with me,
and to all of those families who have lived the reality of a loved one
suffering from mental illness.*

How to Live Like Amy
by Steff Sands

1. Pose for the camera

2. Take WAY too many pictures

3. Dance so that EVERYONE is watching

4. Sing as often as possible

5. Talk in a crazy accent, just for the hell of it

6. Don't make plans for anything

7. Be inappropriately sexy, and don't apologize for it

*8. Accessorize excessively- you can never have too many blinged out rings
or chunky necklaces*

9. Wear hair extensions every day

*10. There is no such thing as too much bronzer, too many false eyelashes, or too
much black eyeliner*

11. Know what you want, and tell people to do things your way

*12. Live life to the fullest, laugh loud, and love deeply,
cuz that's what Amy would do*

Foreword
by Fran L. Porter

Debbie and I met and bonded last year over a tragedy we had experienced in common. That this tragedy has been life-changing for us both has cemented our friendship. We are the mothers of daughters we loved very much but lost to untimely death. And long before that final irrevocable loss occurred, we both had a horrible premonition of the fate awaiting our precious children.

The culprit that so completely robbed and devastated us is a serious mental illness known as borderline personality disorder (BPD). My Colleen, Debbie's Amy, and all who suffer from it (about 2% of the population) are born with a brain dysfunction. But until relatively recently, even experts had scant understanding of its cause and scantier knowledge still about how to treat it. Colleen was born in 1978, Amy in 1984. The society of their childhood and adolescent years was quick to condemn their unruly behaviour, failure to cope with school or home life, flouting of authority, and tendency to a high-risk lifestyle involving drug use and dangerously abusive relationships. And some were even quicker to condemn the parenting skills of mothers whose daughters were so obviously out of control.

Did Debbie and I see ourselves as incompetent parents who maybe did things we shouldn't have, or failed to do things we should have? Did we have doubts about being too strict or too lenient—or just not up to the demands of raising a child? I did, and Debbie assures me she did also. Yet no matter how hard we tried, how many professionals we consulted, or how many strategies we used, nothing was ever enough. Interaction with our daughters—as we have told each other—was often something we dreaded because it involved feelings of anger, frustration and absolute failure to communicate.

Like other mental disorders, BPD is a spectrum disease. Those who have it less severely are able to deal better with life's normal ups and downs; the Colleens and Amys of the world, who have it very severely, find the mere thought of getting through each day an enormous struggle. Keen intelligence often goes hand-in-hand with BPD. From earliest childhood Colleen was instantly able to solve complicated puzzles and grasp higher-level concepts; Debbie has told me similar stories of Amy's brightness. All the more, then, has society been utterly baffled as to why sufferers have such difficulty coping, why significant numbers drop out of school, can't hold jobs, end up on the streets, or land themselves in jail. Make no mistake: whether mild, moderate, or severe, BPD imposes major challenges on all afflicted with it, as well as on the friends, relatives, spouses, co-workers—and yes, parents of those afflicted people.

My husband Andy and I tried repeatedly to get help for Colleen. The moment she was old enough, she refused to keep appointments we made for her with psychiatrists and/or psychotherapists. Besides, those experts frankly admitted, her uncooperative attitude made her very difficult to work with. Debbie and her husband Ed paint the same bleak picture regarding Amy. Both girls grew up at a time when far less understanding existed of why they were so troubled. Ground-breaking work on BPD, begun in the late 1980s, happened too late to save either of them.

Colleen took her life in 2010, driving me to chronicle her tortured journey (When the Ship has no Stabilizers, published March 2014) mainly to help our granddaughter Jaimie—Colleen's daughter, whom we ultimately had to remove from Colleen's care—to better understand the illness that took her mom. Amy's fate, as recounted by Debbie, you will read about within these pages. Both stories are very sad. And yet hope exists today that has never existed before!

Since fMRIs (functional magnetic resonance images), or pictures of the brain at work, have become more readily available, what they have shown us is huge. A mentally-ill brain is not at all like a 'normal' or typical brain. The amygdala at the base of the brain, which controls impulsive urges and emotions, lights up more strongly in a BPD brain. These people experience emotion more intensely than 'regular' people. They might take offense where none is intended. They might succumb to paranoia, seeming malicious because they retaliate against perceived insults. They might binge eat, and then purge after the immediate craving is gone. They might have multiple relationships, both sexual and social, each lasting only briefly. They might be more inclined to shoplift and engage in other criminal behaviours. And—because the disease has no effect on intelligence—they will almost certainly be on a perpetual roller-coaster of elation at gratifying a pleasurable urge, followed by self-hatred when the rational part of the brain again kicks in.

The BPD brain's frontal lobes which govern decision-making and executive thinking—as well as evaluating the consequences of one's own actions—are relatively dimly lit in fMRIs. In other words, a flood of emotion that the BPD sufferer cannot control often drowns out all possibility of rational thinking at the exact time when an appealing urge or a strong desire hits.

What I am saying here is that neither Debbie nor I knew what we were contending with when our daughters were growing up. Statements like 'she has to get real and get her behaviour under control' were commonly uttered to me about Colleen by professionals in the field and by my daughter's teachers. These well-meaning people were equating their own 'take' on the world to Colleen's. (I function all right; why can't she?) What fMRI images show us today is that, mentally, most of us live in a 'normal' world that might be compared to Kansas, and we judge everything from that perspective. BPD sufferers live in Oz. They have no frame of reference to typical 'reality' because they have never known it.

Understanding this has enabled behavioural science at last to move on to the next step: acknowledging that BPD sufferers have a true disability that they—like other disabled people—must and can learn to live with. Today, the 'gold standard' for treating BPD is known as dialectical behaviour therapy (DBT), begun in the late 1980s by behavioural psychologist Marsha Linehan (herself a BPD sufferer!). Enough time has now elapsed since these treatments were first administered to core test-subject groups to show definite changes in the fMRIs of sufferers' brains after DBT has been undergone! The brain, we have learned, possesses an amazing ability known as neuroplasticity: that is, the capacity to re-program itself. With the help of trained experts (which now widely exist) BPD sufferers can employ a regimen designed to 'calm down' the emotionally overactive parts of their brains, allowing reason and judgment to hold more 'normal' sway in their lives' planning and decision-making processes.

Putting it this way makes it sound entirely too simplistic. It isn't. DBT is hard work, and achieving effective results takes self-discipline and patience: two qualities BPD sufferers do not have in abundance. However, more data is being accumulated daily telling us that the BPD life need not be lived in torture and need not end in tragedy, the way Colleen's and Amy's lives did. Telling our daughters' stories is one way that Debbie and I have chosen to help others, help ourselves, and honour the memories of our unfortunate children. If the reader of Debbie's account can view what happened to Amy as a strong case for being proactive about researching and accessing the help that is out there today, then Amy's short life will not have been lived in vain.

CROSSFIELD
PUBLISHING

Amy and Ed Sands, Christmas 2009

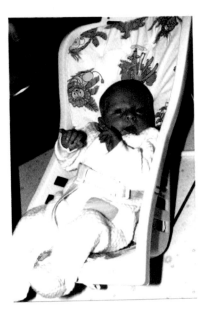

top: Amy at one month, 1984

bottom: Debbie and Amy, 1985

Amy Is Born

This is the story of our middle child, Amy, a beautiful but troubled child, who chose a different path in life from that of her siblings, and from anything we would have hoped for her. The path she went down led to an untimely death, after a life packed with more experiences than many people will witness in a lifetime. She told us, when she was quite young, that she didn't want to live past the age of thirty and that she wanted to die young and beautiful. We never dreamt at the time that her words would be prophetic, and that we would have to live our later years with only her memory, not her presence, in our lives. We think of her every day, and hope that her spirit has found the peace that eluded her in her lifetime.

Amy was born in Calgary during the full moon in November of 1984. The hospital was very busy that night. I had been having regular contractions for a week and was even sent home after thinking I was in labour the weekend before. Then, late in the evening on November 9th, my contractions suddenly got stronger, but irregular. My husband, Ed, was getting ready to take me to the hospital and then the contractions stopped altogether. On the advice of the health nurse we called, I took a hot bath and they resumed not long afterwards, although still irregular.

I walked the halls of the hospital for several hours into the next day and then, all of a sudden, the contractions became so strong that I could no longer walk a few paces without leaning against the wall. Ed told me I should go back to my room and lie down. Sure enough, Amy was on her way, although the contractions remained irregular throughout: the opposite of a normal labour – where contractions are usually irregular with false labour and regular when real labour starts!

After an easy delivery, she came out, crying like any other newborn. As they laid her in my arms, Ed commented. "She looks like a little Ben". Ben was my red-headed father, and my mother was told the very same thing when I was born!

For the next hour, she lay contentedly in my arms but, every time Ed tried to hold her, she would start screaming loudly and "look" across the room (can newborns really see much?) until I took her back. This pattern was to be repeated for the next few days. It seemed odd, but we didn't worry too much about it at the time.

When we got her home, she had given up that habit and would allow her dad to hold her. She was a good baby who mostly slept and ate, actually sleeping through the night at only two weeks of age (and scaring me half to death when I woke up the next morning and hadn't heard her during the night!). I ran into her room, only to see her sleeping peacefully in her crib.

Most of her baby photos during those first few months show her sleeping, and I thanked my lucky stars for such an easy baby. Our first daughter, Stephanie, had been fussy and hadn't slept through the night until four months of age, so I thought Amy was a dream. However, there was something else that we noticed. She would be sitting happily in her little baby chair or swing, cooing and gurgling as babies often do, and then she would suddenly start to scream her head off, turning red and sometimes blue, until someone fed her or put her to bed. By this stage, she would allow anyone to hold her, but her fury at being made to wait more than ten seconds for food or her crib would send us all scurrying! When she graduated to baby food, we would often stand in front of the microwave yelling "Hurry!" as she screamed her lungs out desperately.

Later on, as a very little girl, if she scraped her knees or hit her head on something, she would scream until she was hyperventilating and her eyes would cross. She would start to pass out, until Ed or I urged her, "Breathe, Amy!" We just thought her an extremely sensitive child, and gave it no passing thought. Stephanie was much tougher, but then she always seemed that way.

In 1985, we moved the family to Okotoks, a small town about 20 kilometres south of Calgary. At the time, it had a population of about 3,700 and only one stop light, and we thought it would be a good place in which to raise children. Ed and his business partner had purchased a chiropractic practice there, but the partner had left after only a couple of years. He chose to go back to Calgary and run the business in Midnapore, which the two of them had opened but had struggled with. Ed became the sole owner of the business and, since it came with a ready-made clientele, it helped us through the difficult economic times of the early '80's, when the federal government's "National Energy Programme" had all but destroyed Alberta's thriving oil industry. We were actually able to purchase our first house and move there with the children in June of that year.

The town was very pretty, with one main street of shops and businesses, and several surrounding residential areas. People would often ride their horses down the main street, which you certainly can't do now! Sweeping fields bordered the town, where houses had not yet been built. Today, you will see mostly houses and shopping centres as, 30 years later, it is no longer the little town that we moved to. It was always friendly, though, with a strong emphasis on families, and we had wonderful neighbours and friends. We will probably live here for the rest of our lives as, although it has grown greatly, it still manages to retain its "small town feel".

As Amy grew into a cute and sweet little girl who, when asked if she would like to do something, always replied "Yeah!" and scurried off to do it, she was loving and biddable and we had no problems with her. She did have some food allergies, however, which presented themselves when she started to eat solid food, and they took us a long time to figure out. She was on a very bland diet for many months, but it didn't seem to affect her happy mood at that age. She and her sister bonded right from the start, and Stephanie showed no jealousy of her. They played together all day long. When we moved to Okotoks, the little girl next door, Amelia, would come over and the three of them would play dress-up and fairy tale characters all day long. Later on, three friends playing together would always be disastrous for Amy.

Amy went to playschool at age three, and was a favourite with the teachers. However, her vivid imagination would get her into trouble sometimes! One day, she told me that her little buddy's mom, my friend Rosie, had brought peanut butter sandwiches for snack. I said to Amy, "Oh no, doesn't Rosie know that Charles is allergic to peanut butter?" Amy replied, "Yes, and he started to choke and make funny noises. The ambulance had to come!" The next day, I asked Rosie what she was thinking making peanut butter sandwiches, and she looked at me as though I had two heads!

"I didn't make peanut butter snacks – I know Charles is allergic to it!" She replied defensively. Amy's teachers later told me to only believe half of what I heard from playschool, and they would only believe half of what they heard from home!

When she turned four, I was pregnant with our son Michael. One day, I asked Amy to do something and she stamped her foot, turned around and glared at me. "No!" She shouted. That was the first time she ever defied me, and little did I know it was only the beginning of a very long journey of defiance and stubbornness. I don't even remember what it was about, but I remember that day as though it were yesterday.

Her behaviour had started to change somewhat, and she would often feel "unfairness" when playing with Stephanie and Amelia. She would come to me and tell me that the other girls were being "mean" to her, and I would have to go and talk to them about it. They always seemed unaware that they had been treating her any differently from normal.

I remember my friend, Carla (who was also Stephanie's godmother), was babysitting our girls once while we were away for a few days. She told me that Amy was one day lying across the bed, her head resting on her hands, with big tears in her eyes, telling her that the other kids were being unkind to her. They hadn't done anything so terrible that Carla could figure out! This was starting to be a pattern when Amy was playing with other children, and would continue throughout her childhood.

Michael was born the following February, and he entered the world as the baby brother of two happy little sisters. Stephanie was often stubborn, and could be quite difficult sometimes when she had her mind made up about something, but the rest of the time she was a good little girl who played happily with her sister. Amy was becoming more stubborn, but I thought at the time that she was only mirroring her sister's behaviour. And they both knew how to manipulate! When we tried to go out, I would often have a little girl holding onto each of my legs, begging me not to leave them with the babysitter. Apparently, as soon as we left, they would turn to the sitter and say, "Okay, let's play!" I would meanwhile be beating myself up for abandoning my children, and we couldn't enjoy our evening out!

Michael was a good baby, who was so serene that he didn't even seem to hear the girls playing noisily. I worried about his hearing, but was assured by the doctor that he wasn't deaf, just content! Amy never showed any jealousy of him at that stage, and often tried to "help" me by picking him up and bringing him to me. My heart in my mouth, I'd say "Thank you, honey!" as I scooped him up from his sister's arms. Later on, she would become savagely jealous of him and would often beat him up and threaten him when we weren't home.

When Amy turned five, she went to kindergarten. We had thought about holding her back because her birthday was in November, but she was so anxious to go to school like her big sister that we decided against it. I must admit that having one child less to look after for a couple of hours in the afternoon was also rather appealing, and I could get housework done or take a nap while the girls were at school. I will always remember seeing the two little girls walking home from school holding hands, among all their friends, as I walked up to meet them on the corner.

Amy was one of the most popular girls in her class in kindergarten and also in grade one. Her outgoing personality and vibrant imagination made her the centre of attention during playtime and recess, and she always had children around her. Her best friends were Allison and Molly, and she had quite a crush on a little boy named Kevin. We had all of them, plus a half a dozen others, over to our new house when she turned six. It was a fun party and her lovely teacher, Mrs. Baker, phoned to wish her a happy birthday! Amy was so happy that day.

top: "Posing" for the first day of kindergarten, Sept. 1989.

bottom: Amy in grade 5, taken at home

Later Elementary School

Life continued on and the children grew bigger. By grade 4, everything had changed for Amy. She had started to put on weight and, due to a lazy eye, had to wear corrective glasses. By grade 6, she needed braces on her teeth because of an overbite. She was no longer the cute little girl she had been in kindergarten, and wasn't popular any more. By this time, she disliked school and actually hated math She was helped by an education assistant in grade 5 and, with her dad's supplementary help, she was more or less able to keep up.

Due to her problems, she had developed the reputation for being "stupid" in school, and was teased mercilessly by the "mean" kids. She still had her best friends, Allison and Molly, but the dynamics between the three of them had changed. They no longer played happily for hours, sometimes involving Stephanie in their play. There was a constant tug of war between Amy and Molly, usually over Allison's friendship, and it caused Amy a lot of heartache when Molly temporarily won.

Amy was becoming a much unhappier child by this stage, often defiant and difficult, taking offense easily at the slightest little thing, and having to be grounded or sent to her room many times. I have to admit that we even resorted to spanking once in a while. My parents had done it to me, and I figured that I turned out all right! I was brought up strictly, and I tried to be more indulgent with my kids, reading all the psychology magazines and books about giving children choices and "negotiating" with them, instead of disciplining. Unfortunately, I sometimes lost my patience and resorted to the old-fashioned methods! The debate is still out on that issue.

By grade six, Amy was really struggling in school. The Alberta Premier at the time, Ralph Klein, had introduced cutbacks to education and healthcare, in an effort to reduce the provincial deficit. This impacted our family on two fronts – Ed, as a chiropractor, was the main source of our family's income, and we had to constantly pay extra fees to the school system. I started to work more at Ed's office to help out with our family's financial situation.

Note: She likely inherited her difficulty in math from me – I needed a tutor to get through my school exams.

On the education side, the aide that Amy had for math was laid off, and it was now only we who could help her with her homework. Ed had far more patience than me, but even he got testy at her inability to focus and to apply herself. She seemed to be obsessed with TV and was constantly asking for a video game console to play with. Knowing her inability to get her homework done before turning to recreation, we forbade her the game console and refused to buy her one for her birthday when she asked for one. It was only later on, when Michael got himself a part-time job and saved up all his birthday money and allowance that one came into our house. I also tried to curtail Amy's TV watching by cutting the cable for a couple of years, so the other kids were unfairly punished for her refusal to comply and do her homework! It was only the first of many things that the other two children were forced to endure because of her behaviour.

On a positive note, though, Amy had always exhibited a talent for dressing up and imitating movie characters and fairy tale folk. She also had a strong little singing voice, and loved to pose for pictures as many different characters (usually from Disney movies). Ed had a patient who ran a theatre group, which often performed plays with kids, and the lady suggested he bring her to an audition. She was immediately cast in the children's play, and even given a duet to sing with another little girl, and that was the start of a deep internal passion for theatre. She played many parts over the years, always with a talent and brilliance that was enviable. We also volunteered to help out with the production, and that started off an interest in theatre for our whole family, which continues to this day, although Stephanie eventually preferred to do the hair and makeup and Mike liked to play music.

By grade 6, Amy was deeply unhappy at school. There was a boy in her class, I'll call him Cory, who became her nemesis and teased her mercilessly every day. He picked on many other kids, but Amy was his favourite target. He was a charismatic, short little guy whose air of bravado and defiance won him the admiration of the other pre-pubescent boys, and they joined him in making Amy's life at school unbearable. I once complained about him to the homeroom teacher, saying that he'd said "horrible things" about Amy, and the teacher replied that he was a "horrible boy, but there was nothing she could do about it". She said that he liked to tease other kids if they were bugging him, but Amy only had to walk across the classroom and he would start on her, encouraging the other kids to join in. She also commented that that whole year of kids was very difficult, and that the teachers dreaded teaching them as they came up through the elementary school.

By this time, Amy was becoming very "different" from a lot of kids her age, being artistic and eccentric in her tastes. It was very noticeable. Children this age love to pick on the outsider, and bullies like Cory took special delight in tormenting them.

Amy was by now a very angry and unhappy girl, fighting with us on a regular basis and refusing to do her homework. There were frequent arguments with Allison and Molly, too, which forced the parents to get involved and, at one point, Molly's mom and I cooled our friendship because she blamed Amy for mistreating her daughter. We never found out all the facts, but apparently the mistreatment was mutual!

One day, while cleaning, I found a note in Amy's room. I think it was a poem – I don't remember the gist of it, but the things that stuck in my mind were the words "death", "funeral" and "black". I came to the terrible conclusion that our little girl was deeply depressed, and the contents of the note really concerned me. A wonderful woman in Okotoks, Donna, had started up a small private school for gifted children and I talked to Ed about getting Amy into the school, as it also took kids who were struggling in the public system, and there were no entrance exams. Due to the provincial cutbacks, we weren't in a position to afford it but my parents, who were great believers in education and had sent my brothers and me to private schools in England, agreed to help.

Amy's fascination with the colour black and other sinister things continued throughout her teenage years and early adulthood, and may have been a signal of what was to come. But we didn't know that at the time.

Note: Cory grew up to be a rebellious teenager who indulged in reckless behaviour. On his seventeenth birthday, he and his buddy got drunk in a hotel room and stole the buddy's mom's car, driving it down a steep hill in Okotoks and eventually smashing into a tree. Cory was seriously injured, and was taken off life support a week later. Another senseless tragedy that stemmed from poor choices!

Amy at private school, grade 7

Junior High

Amy started at the private school in the fall of 1996, and was quite happy there for the first two years. However, she still didn't understand math and gave her teacher a very hard time. Poor Mr. Liu, it was his first year of teaching, and he did his best, but she defied him often and disrupted his class at times. She would then end up in the principal's office and we would get a call. We tried to help her at home, but her inability to focus caused frustration. We wondered whether she had attention deficit disorder (ADD), but most of her teachers disagreed. One teacher suggested that we have her tested but, with Ed being in a holistic profession, we felt that that would then lead to her being put on Ritalin, and we didn't believe in medicating young children unless they had a medical problem. (Looking back, maybe it would have helped her, but we know of several kids who ended up selling their Ritalin on the streets, and I'm not sure she wouldn't have done that, given the path that her life eventually took.)

By now, Amy was turning twelve. She was involved at this point in her life in theatre, singing lessons, dance, and karate, and had also done swimming and baton-twirling at various times. We tried to keep all of our kids involved in extracurricular activities, although money was often tight. Stephanie played the piano, danced and did baton-twirling and gymnastics. Mike played the guitar (and was quite a virtuoso, who continued on into a career in music), but all three had little interest in sports (like their parents!). Mike did karate, swim club and played football during junior high and high school. He also tried hockey, but he gave them all up in favour of playing his guitar.

As teenagehood approached, hormones kicked in and Amy became more and more difficult. The mood swings were horrendous, and her anger could often become violent. She fought with us constantly, often over homework or the performance of chores, and was very defiant any time we tried to discipline her. In fact, I often used to joke, "If you try to stop Amy from doing what she wants, you'll have a fight on your hands. Also, if you try to make Amy do something she doesn't want to do, you'll have a fight on your hands." It wasn't really a joke, just a statement of fact, but I always said it with a grim smile on my face!

By this stage, she was picking on Michael mercilessly, although it was always done while we were at work or out of the house. She was also becoming an accomplished liar, and would steal any money that was left lying around. However, she was still a very loving girl who was fiercely loyal to her friends. She and Stephanie were still close at this point, and shared each other's secrets. School was becoming more difficult, as she navigated the waters of "mean girls" and boys who mocked her for her weight and for being slow at math. She had started to gravitate towards the "bad girls" from Calgary who had been sent by their parents to the Okotoks private school to try and straighten them out.

She and I would get into arguments, usually about some disciplinary issue, and I wouldn't always exercise patience or restraint. Instead of telling her the rules, then giving her a consequence to the disobedience and walking away, I would stand and argue with her, our voices rising by the minute. The fight would go on and on, each one of us trying to get the last word, and it would usually end in tears on her side, and fury on mine. Many times, Ed told me to just walk away, and I even ended up taking an anger management course to teach me how to deal with my anger. I'm afraid I never followed the advice that was given and would continue to have the screaming fights with her. I sometimes did it with Stephanie, too (though Michael was usually pretty biddable, and didn't need a raised voice – he took his consequences patiently!) and this became a bad pattern for our family. Many a time I had to close the windows in the summer, so the neighbours wouldn't hear the screaming. I had reaped the results of earlier on trying to be my children's friend, instead of their parent, and both girls were starting to disrespect me greatly, although Amy more so than Stephanie.

Grade 9 is when things really started to unravel at home. Amy by now was skipping class on a regular basis, hanging out behind the school with her delinquent friends and drinking alcohol. She had two good friends, Jordan and Ashley, and they contributed to her delinquency. They were all boy-crazy, and it was around this age (14) that we learned through a family friend with a child in the know that Amy had met a boy at a party and lost her virginity. This was the start of a long history of boyfriends and promiscuity, usually involving drinking or drugs. Her marks plummeted, and the teachers at the school would suspend her regularly, asking us to pick her up from school. Since we were both working, I felt that allowing her to come home for the day to do whatever she felt like wasn't a punishment, and that the teachers should keep her in the office doing schoolwork. I do believe they were doing their best with the resources they had to help kids like her, but Amy was wanting to return to the mainstream school system.

The Foothills Composite High School in Okotoks had a very highly-regarded drama programme (called "Mainstage" at that time), with a wonderful teacher, and she wanted to be a part of that. Theatre was still her first love. She had played many wonderful roles, and went on to play several in the high school, though mostly just in the chorus in the Mainstage programme. It was in the Studio Theatre programme that she excelled; she did a particularly wonderful job of the role of the Nurse in "Romeo and Juliet". Her talent for comedic timing was very much in evidence!

I remember her playing the role of a maid in one of our theatre group's productions, a J. B. Priestley play called "When We Are Married". She put on a Cockney accent, and was dressed in an adorable dress and cap, which suited her very well. She was perky and clever in the role, and managed to "ad lib" one day so that the audience never even noticed when Ed, who was supposed to be acting in the scene with her, forgot his cue and didn't arrive until two or three minutes after his entrance. The audience never suspected!

So it happened that, by grade 10, she returned to the public school system to pursue her love of theatre. She was very excited about it. Her relationship with Stephanie was still fairly strong, although she had started stealing her sister's clothes and makeup from her room, and this caused a lot of uproar!

top: High school graduation, 2003

bottom: Amy as "Ruby" in J.B. Priestly's "When We Are Married, 2003

*top: Stephanie, Michael and Amy with their grandparents taken on
Ed's 50th birthday, 2003*

bottom: last formal family photo, Debbie, Amy, Ed, Michael, and Stephanie, 2000

The reader may wonder why our last "official" family photo was taken when the girls were teenagers, and Michael was still very young. Well, the problem lay mostly in trying to get the whole family together at any given time!

Stephanie was in Grade 12 at the time this picture from 2000 was taken, and she left home about two years after that. She went on to college for a few months, then started hairdressing and moved in with her future husband shortly after that. Amy, by that time, was running with her fast crowd, and was often not home at weekends or in the evenings. Ed was also very busy with work and town council obligations, so the amount of planning and organization it would take to book an appointment time for a family photo, and then to get everyone to actually show up, was minimal. With only Michael and me consistently at home, it was difficult to get the whole group together for the "family photo"! It was something we always meant to do, but time just got away on us.

The other, more ominous omission, is many photos of Amy and me together, other than when she was a small child. By the time she was a teenager, she and I were fighting constantly over everything. I was the parent who was mostly at home, and therefore the disciplinarian. Amy always made it her mission to oppose anything I said, or any rules I tried to impose, so there was a lot of discord in our house. By the time she had moved out, we were no longer arguing on a daily basis, but there were still many unpleasant incidents, mostly due to our opposition to her drug use.

We did have a family photo of all of us together at Stephanie's wedding, but the picture includes Stephanie's husband, therefore won't be used in these pages. However, I am completely challenged to find any of just Amy and me by ourselves. Ed was usually the photographer, and maybe he found it best to not invite the two of us to pose together, for fear of a fight breaking out over poses or one person not being willing to have their picture taken. It is a source of great regret to me in looking back, and I wish that we had been more cognizant of it at the time.

High School

Amy thought she could go to high school and be a part of the "cool group". She was still overweight and had endured some teasing and difficult friendships at the private school, but the teachers kept a close eye on this and usually dealt with the problems. However, in the public system, there were just too many kids, and they couldn't deal with individual situations. She soon discovered that the "cool girls" didn't want to be her friends. She was back to being the outcast, and even the drama kids weren't very accepting of her. Her kind heart caused her to be nice to other girls who were left out, but even they weren't always accepting of her! Poor Amy just couldn't understand why the kids wouldn't let her be a part of their group, even though her sister had endured the same thing for being overweight (although shy and quiet) and knew what it was all about. Stephanie reacted by turning inwards and seeking out other quiet, shy girls, but Amy reacted in the way that she always had, with anger and rebelliousness.

She soon joined the "skid" kids. These were usually underprivileged kids from lower socio-economic backgrounds, and several of the boys were already "B and E artists". (break and enter). Instead of being frowned upon, they were usually admired by this group, and emulated. She started to dress like them, adopting "Goth" clothing, usually wearing black outfits with long, baggy pants that showed her underwear. Amy always told me that she liked being a part of this group, because they never judged her.

There was also a history of drinking in public among these kids, and using drugs. It wasn't very long before she began indulging in this, too – the kids used to drink down in the local park by the river, and were often arrested for being intoxicated in public. Marijuana was smoked, and "magic mushrooms" consumed, and I don't know exactly when she started smoking pot, but she was already smoking cigarettes by this age (as was her sister).

One day, we got a call from the drama teacher at the high school, whom I'll call Mr. Spencer. He told us that Amy had been bragging about going to smoke pot with one of the school "cool" guys and that one of the students had ratted her out. He wanted to suspend her from the drama programme, and wanted Ed and me to be brought in for a discussion about it. Apparently, Amy's reply was, "No, please, don't tell my mum!"

By this point, she and I had a fraught relationship - I was trying to be the strict parent, and grounding her frequently for bad behaviour and defiance of the house rules. I don't know whether she was afraid of me, or whether she loved me enough to want to protect me from the things she was doing, but she certainly didn't want Mr. Spencer to tell me what she'd been up to!

The end result was that Amy wasn't suspended, but had to promise to toe the line and submit to regular drug testing (it was never done). She applied herself fairly well to her role in the drama programme after that and participated successfully in a musical that the school put on. We were so proud of her when she sang in the chorus of the play in her peasant costume!

She did jeopardize her acting, however, during a production by our theatre group of a nineteenth-century musical in which she had been given a solo singing role. She practiced her song diligently, and really enjoyed being with the kids who were in the play with her. However, three days before the opening night, she announced that she was going to get her tongue pierced! I reacted with horror.

"Amy," I said in a severe tone of voice, "whatever you do, do NOT get your tongue pierced! They didn't do that in the nineteenth century, and everyone will see it when you open your mouth to sing. Besides, you have to be over 18 or have permission to get piercings!"

We were in the car at the time and, sure enough, she got out at the nearest light, slammed the door and walked off, only to return that night with a pierced tongue. I immediately called the director and music director of the show (I was the producer) and we all agreed, as did Ed, that she should be pulled from the show. She needed to have a consequence to her defiant action. The other actors were very upset and begged us to keep Amy, as they all loved her. We held strong for the first week, and an understudy took her part. However, we all caved after that and allowed her back onstage. We figured that she had endured enough punishment. Whether this was the right thing to do, or whether it just gave her the message that you can break the rules and then be allowed to do whatever you want after a short period, is something that I've wrestled with ever since.

We had all continued to work in theatre, Ed and I in the production and drama ends of things, while Amy played many roles in our amateur group. She acted mostly supporting roles at first, then some lead roles, like the Princess in "Aladdin". Ed had taken on many supporting roles and so had I, since I had been afraid to even go on the stage until I was nearly 50! However, one year, I got to play "Lady Bracknell" in "The Importance of Being Earnest", and that was so much fun for me, as well as being the biggest role that I have ever taken on. Theatre (and especially comedy) continued to be our therapy throughout Amy's teen years, and probably helped to lessen our stress somewhat. The amazing support and sense of family that the theatre group conveyed was a great help to us during those difficult times.

In the summer of 1999, when Amy was fifteen, we took the kids to Europe to visit my parents who had a house there. Neither of the girls wanted to go, as they didn't want to leave their friends behind, and we wouldn't allow them to smoke cigarettes (which both were doing at this point, mostly behind our backs) on the trip. After the first week, however (probably due to nicotine withdrawal!), their angry protests and non-stop arguing subsided and they really enjoyed the holiday. Amy later wrote in a school journal that the trip had allowed her to "reconnect with my family". All three of the kids were great for the balance of the trip and we were proud of them. My mum even told me, years later, that she found that the kids were very well-behaved at that time.

However, by this time, Stephanie was starting to have trouble with several of her friends and was also experimenting with alcohol and drugs. She wasn't really overweight, but she also wasn't stick-thin either, and took a fair amount of rude comments from her peers. She at one point tried not eating all day at school and then purging in the evenings after dinner, in an effort to lose weight. Amy, who could never keep secrets to herself if it involved other people, told me what her sister was doing, and I got Stephanie in to see a public health nurse. They had a couple of consultations, and the nurse warned her of the dangers of bulimia. Stephanie then seemed to drop the habit, but was always looking for quick, easy ways of losing weight. She was quite particular in her taste in food, and preferred high-fat, high-carb foods, so was constantly fighting a losing battle!

Amy, too, was dealing with weight issues. Her lessons in karate had taught her how to defend herself against teasing and she was now doing ballet and jazz, as was Stephanie, but they both continued to be bigger than the girls in their dance classes. By the next summer, Amy suddenly dropped about 30 lbs. and, when questioned, told us that she spent the summer walking all over Okotoks and eating only pizza. We believed her, and had no idea about the drugs she had starting using to control her appetite! It was only later that we learned that dexadrine was the reason for the sudden weight loss – it wasn't anorexia, as some people suspected, as she continued to eat well most of the time.

Amy blossomed into a beautiful young girl. Even when she was overweight, she had an exquisite face, and had started wearing contact lenses, so no more glasses. We also took all three kids in for orthodontic treatment, and she was now sporting a dazzling smile with white, straight teeth. She wore her hair long most of the time but, several months before we went to Europe, she had dyed it green for St. Patrick's Day, in spite of express orders from school that that was not allowed. She, of course, defied the rule and dyed her hair anyway! The result (on top of the suspension from school) was that she couldn't get the dye out of her hair. I took her to a hairdresser, who advised that cutting the hair really short was the only way to get rid of the green dye. She came out of the salon with a pixie cut that really suited her face, but she hated it! She spent the rest of the year growing it long again and started dying it blond, perhaps to look like her sister. That was the start of many years of dying her hair blond, then dark, then back to blond again. Her hair was always damaged!

At this point, things had become really difficult at home. Amy's behaviour was now almost uncontrollable. She had no interest in her schoolwork, unless it was drama or sewing class (for which she had also shown considerable talent), and had to be held to the grindstone to get her homework done. This caused more friction between us, although Ed tried to help out occasionally – he had become a town councilor several years before and, what with that and his work as a chiropractor, was often out of the house. I had decided to leave behind the childrearing methods I had read about in some parenting books, (negotiating and giving choices), as clearly it wasn't working, and adopt strict discipline, which was how I was raised. However, I found it hard to be really tough, and often gave in to keep peace in the house! The two girls quickly figured this out, and would push me to the limit until I gave in out of exasperation. Getting them to do chores had become next to impossible and, although Stephanie respected their curfew, Amy didn't and often stayed out way past the acceptable hour, earning herself yet another grounding.

She had also developed a filthy mouth and employed swear words at every opportunity. I threatened her many times, going so far as to wash her mouth out with soap and water and threatening physical punishment, but to no avail. She seemed incapable of controlling her speech.

Inappropriate behaviour was something that dogged her more and more as she grew older. Stephanie felt that she could get away with it, too, and her language became bad also. Michael later would develop a swearing habit, and maybe it's just part of the younger generation's way of expressing themselves, but my strict upbringing caused me to find this really distasteful. Neither of her siblings swore as indiscriminately as Amy. The constant family arguments were weighing everyone down and causing lots of stress, so I eventually sought out a local psychologist, Dr. Harris, to help me deal with Amy's behaviour.

When she was fifteen, she and Stephanie started hanging out at a house that was designated the "crack house" in Okotoks. It wasn't really a crack house, but they and the other "skid" kids often went there to drink and smoke pot. One evening, Amy went there and stayed out all night! She was instantly grounded for the next two weeks, and I talked to her about why she did it. During the course of the discussion, she said, "Mum, while I was sleeping, I woke up and there was a boy with his hand up my shirt!"

I panicked and immediately made an appointment with the psychologist to try to figure out how to stop her from sneaking out at night and going there. She talked to Dr. Harris first about it, then I went in with him and I told him that I had grounded her for staying out all night.

His reply was, "You are too strict with her. Because of your authoritarian ways, she is acting out. If you want peace in your house, you need to let Amy do what she wants."

I was flabbergasted! I couldn't believe what I was hearing. I told him that I'd read several books on dealing with difficult kids, and they all advocated boundaries for rebellious teenagers. Not giving them a curfew and allowing them to do what they wanted was exactly what caused them to act out more. Also, I couldn't let Amy continue to go to that house and possibly end up getting raped! He disagreed with me, and we never went back to see him again. Of course, Amy liked the fact that he encouraged letting her do whatever she wanted, and was mad at me for discontinuing the visits.

After one particularly traumatic fight between us, during which she called me every name under the sun and told me I was crazy, I ended up in tears at the local health unit, requesting to see the mental health professional. The kind assistant, who knew Ed through a service organization, was very sweet to me. This made me cry even more, and I was in a state by the time I saw the psychologist. She turned out to be a lovely lady named Maria, and the first thing she did after hearing my story was to assure me that I wasn't crazy, but that the situation I was living with was crazy!

I felt such relief at being understood by another adult. For a couple of years now, I had been starting to believe that maybe there was something wrong with me – my inability to control my two daughters and my fury at their refusal to listen to me or do anything I asked them was causing me a lot of stress. In addition, Amy's violent temper, her crying jags and firm belief that everyone in her family hated her and that all the world (except her skid friends) hated her too, was causing our family life to be a rollercoaster of anger and self-doubt.

Maria understood a lot of the issues, and was patient and gentle with Amy, as well as being kind and supportive to Ed, who had been brought in on some of the visits, and to me. I don't think I remember any sessions with the whole family and, looking back, perhaps that would have been a good idea. We were only allowed eight sessions with Maria through Alberta Health Care but, because Ed was on Town Council, we now had medical benefits, and our visits with her were mostly covered. Things didn't exactly calm down at home, but they improved for a while. Unfortunately, Maria then moved into Calgary, and we no longer had the time or the motivation to go and see her there.

The Goth bedroom

Amy, circa 2001

Amy at the Mainstage Gala, Foothills Composite
High School, grade 11

New Figures In Our Lives

Things were starting to change in our household. We acquired a boarder – a lovely boy named David, who lived with us for four years altogether. He came from a close-knit family, and had come to Okotoks to attend the high school drama programme.

Mr. Spencer had decided to take a sabbatical and teach in another city for a year. At the end of the year, he returned to our school, bringing several students with him. He needed to find homes for these students and asked us whether we would have David, as we lived only ten minutes from the school, and he liked our family. I hesitated, because I felt that a stranger shouldn't have to put up with the constant family fights and lack of structure that our household had deteriorated into because of Amy's behaviour. However, David came to town with his parents during the school holidays, and we all fell in love! The kids got along great with each other, and Ed and I immediately liked and respected his parents. His mother was a guidance counselor, and I felt that he would be a good kid who would have a good influence on our children.

David certainly was a good influence on Michael, as well as being a "big brother" to him. He seemed to really like us, and we never had an ounce of trouble with him. He respected our house rules, and always behaved in an exemplary way with us. He's still welcome at our house any time, and we love to go and visit his family any time we're in their home town.

I later found out that, on his first night in Okotoks, Amy took David and his friend to a party, where she immediately got them drunk! David went upstairs to throw up, then ended up passing out in one of the bedrooms of the house. Apparently, a girl at the party had thought him very cute, and followed him upstairs. She tried to get into bed with him, but Miss Amy figured out what was going on! She ran into the room and screamed at the girl to "leave him alone and get out!" She championed her new "little brother's" virginity, even though she had thrown her own away at a party a couple of years before.

Amy's relationships with boys were usually short-lived and she didn't have any steady boyfriends at this stage. She did meet a very nice boy when she was sixteen, whom I will call Justin, as he reminded me very much of Justin Timberlake when he had his curly hair. Justin was a nice boy from a good family, and he lived in Calgary. He and his friends were very different from Amy's, and I think it was that difference that attracted him to her. He became quite besotted with her, and I met him on a couple of occasions at our house. I commented to Amy that he was a "very nice boy", and that was probably the kiss of death! She told me that his friends' girlfriends were "snotty" to her, and that they made her feel uncomfortable. I encouraged her to keep seeing him, but she had other plans.

He called our house one day, just before Valentine's Day, and I answered the phone He told me excitedly about the plans that he had for "his girl" for the big day, and it certainly was very nice. A romantic dinner in a fancy restaurant – most of Amy's friends at that stage of her life certainly couldn't have afforded such a treat.

Well, I learned shortly after that she had dumped the poor boy right on Valentine's Day! I couldn't believe that she could be so heartless, but I guess I should have realized that she would have little interest in a boy of whom her mother approved.

In grade 12, Amy began dating Luke, who was one of the "skid" boys who hung out at the park. He seemed like a nice enough boy, with a beautiful smile, although he had a difficult relationship with his parents. He was the father of a little boy, but had never paid any child support to the boy's mother, so had had his driver's license and social security card confiscated by the government. He certainly was more Amy's type than poor Justin had been!

That summer, Luke came to live with us. His mother had finally kicked him out for his behaviour and Amy begged us to let him stay with us. I was very reluctant, but told her that he could stay in the basement for a few days, as long as he promised to go back and talk to his mom. Amy had to sleep in her own room at the top of the house, and she wasn't allowed to tiptoe down to the basement after we were asleep!

Every day that summer, I told Luke to go and talk to his mom. He always replied that he couldn't talk to her, because she was "crazy". I fell for his story, and believed that she was an abusive parent, because I had only heard his and Amy's side of things. (We later met his parents and found them to be lovely people, who definitely had their children's welfare at heart – they had only been practicing "tough love".) In his defense, though, he behaved extremely well at our house – he was always respectful and polite to us, even helping with chores and getting Amy to do the same. He brought some measure of peace to our house, maybe partly because he kept Amy busy and often out of the house. He did eventually make up with his parents and move back home.

More Rebellious Behaviour

In the spring of grade 12, Amy and I had had a fight about something – I don't even remember what it was, but it could have been the time that she went out with some friends on a week night, promising to be home by 10 p.m. Well, 10 o'clock came and went, as did 11 o'clock and then midnight. By then, I was frantically calling her on her cell phone and being hung up on many times. I finally told her that she would be grounded for a month and got hung up on again, after being called an unforgiveable name. She, in fact, didn't come home at all that night and didn't even return the next day.

When I eventually got hold of her, she told me that she was "never coming home, as the rules are so stupid!" I was devastated, as the one thing I had been trying really hard to do was to keep her in school so that she could graduate. On the second or third day, I got a call from one of her teachers, asking me to come in to the school and see her. When I got there, she told me that Amy hadn't turned in an assignment that was due. I informed her uncomfortably that Amy had left home and announced her intention of never returning. She was being aided and abetted by Luke, who said that he was spending time with her where she was staying "to protect her", so I didn't see any chance of getting her back any time soon.

The teacher was very supportive, and even admitted that she had had trouble with one of her own children. It was nice to feel understood by an education professional and to know that this wasn't unusual for kids at that age. However, I really hoped Amy would change her mind and come home.

Sure enough, after one week of being away and even meeting with her and Luke and trying to convince her to come back (this was met with determined protests that she would never come back!), I got a call to say that she had bronchitis. It was cold in the house, and nobody had any money to buy her medication, so she came back, a bit chastened, but still difficult any time we tried to impose rules on her.

Her behaviour throughout her teenage years continually puzzled us. She was so up and down with her moods, and sometimes the slightest thing would send her off the deep end into a violent temper. At other times, she would be happy and even-keel about everything. At one point,

Michael asked me if I thought she was bipolar. I told him that bipolar sufferers usually go through long periods of manic behavior, followed by a lengthy episode of depression, and this didn't seem to apply to Amy. Her moods seemed to be subject to quicksilver change, and she didn't suffer from the troughs of depression, as far as I could see. She just didn't fit the picture for that disorder, but we were starting to think that she did show signs of some kind of mental illness. At the time, though, we felt that her psychologists would have picked up on what it was, if anything.

Ed and I were both stressed out by her behaviour. I had developed a habit of grinding my teeth and had even broken three of them, due to the stress. The dentist at one time told me that I could "either move to Hawaii, or have the source of the stress removed". Little did he know that the source was my teenaged middle child! The one thing I am grateful for, though, is that Ed and I were always on the same page about how to deal with Amy and, as stressful as those times were, it didn't eat away at our marriage, the way it so often does with parents of difficult children. He has always been, and continues to be, my rock.

Exercise had also become a big part of my life, ever since Stephanie was a toddler and I realized that, since I hadn't done any aerobic exercise or sport since high school, I could no longer keep up with an active almost two year-old! My friend, Carla, was doing "aerobic dance" at the time and so I took a page out of her book and signed up for classes. I quickly learned to love the extra energy that a day begun with exercise gave me, and also the fact that it helped me to control my weight and to be able to eat pretty much what I wanted (that was true at that age, not so much later!). I am convinced that aerobic exercise, combined with our involvement in community theatre, helped me to cope with the stress of dealing with Amy's behavior. The endorphins released in my body gave me a sense of well-being, and the support network of the ladies in the classes was also very helpful.

I also started power-walking with a friend, Sandy, who had been a social worker before becoming a full-time mom. She was very good at asking me the right questions about my chaotic life with my daughter, and often gave me reassurance and advice on how to cope. At my 50th birthday party, I credited her with helping me get through the stressful times with Amy (and Stephanie, too!).

I haven't mentioned the fact that both of our girls had had part-time jobs since their early teens, as they both liked to wear designer clothes and Ed and I couldn't afford to buy them at that time. We probably wouldn't have bought them for them, anyway, as we felt that they should be satisfied with the less expensive clothes that I purchased for them. Their jobs were supposed to supplement their allowances, so that they could contribute to half of the price of the designer clothes. (This was the early '90's, when materialism and brand snobbery were very common, even among school-age kids.) Well, Stephanie always kept her jobs, and was considered a valuable employee everywhere she went. Amy, on the other hand, always managed to get fired for being late, or for doing the job half-heartedly, or for lying. Michael seemed to follow Stephanie's example and always had a good work ethic, which earned him the respect of his employers. Poor Amy, however, went through many different jobs throughout high school, but always with the same result! I should mention, though, that every time she lost a job, she always said it was because the boss was an "idiot" and didn't understand her own motivations in whatever situation presented itself.

The next summer, Amy had again been fired from a job, but Luke (whom she was still dating) had apparently found one with a construction company. She said she no longer needed to work, as Luke was making a lot of money and was buying her nice things. Every day, she would get up late and go and meet Luke. The weather was beautiful that summer, and the two of them would go down to the river in the late morning and stay there for a while, then Luke would go off to work.

I was starting to smell a rat! The thought occurred to me, "Who works in construction and starts work half-way through the day in the summer?" He must be doing something other than construction, and it was probably illegal, considering how much cash he always seemed to have. Every time I asked her which company he was working for, she'd get really mad and start yelling at me. However, one day, she finally let slip who he was working for. I had also been asking around among some of David's friends as to whether Luke might be involved in some illegal activity. Sure enough, one of them told me that he had seen the wads of money in Luke's wallet when they were at a party and that it was ill-gotten gains from selling pot. So I took matters into my own hands and phoned the construction company that he was supposedly working for. Needless to say, they had never heard of him!

"So, Amy", I said to her later that day when she returned from hanging out with him. "When did Luke start selling drugs down at the river?"

Amy looked completely bowled over. Then she turned on me and screamed at me that he wasn't selling drugs, and how dare I accuse him. I held firm and let her know that his "construction company" had never heard of him. She then started on a huge rant about me and my snooping ways, calling me every name she could think of, then accused me of hating her and trying to make her life miserable. I walked away, after telling her that I was probably going to go to the police about Luke's drug-dealing.

Unfortunately, I didn't follow through on my threat. We had company arriving from Europe a few days later and I didn't want to cause any scenes while they were staying with us. However, little did I know it, but one of the worst scenes of my life was about to play out while they were visiting us.

One afternoon in July, Ed decided to take our German friends for a ride in the country to show them some of the beautiful scenery that abounds in the Banff and Kananaskis areas. I had opted not go with them, but rather to stay home and prepare appetizers and dinner for our guests when they got back. I was to regret that choice later, as it turned out! Amy and I were the only ones in the house, and she was up in her room while I cooked in the kitchen.

At one point, I heard her talking on the phone, hang up and then come downstairs.

"Mum!" she said. "Luke wants to know who told you that he was selling drugs down by the river."

"Amy," I replied, "you know I never reveal my sources."

It had been almost a family joke that, whenever our kids were in trouble and I seemed to know things that I couldn't possibly have known from them, that I would play newspaper reporter and say that I never reveal my sources. Sometimes I had just guessed what was going on, but sometimes I had been tipped off by one of their friends. In this case, I wasn't about to get David's friend in trouble, or subjected to a possible beating by a group of skid boys (he was a big guy who played football, though, so I probably needn't have worried about him – he could take care of himself!).

Amy immediately got mad and started to badger me about it. She said Luke had told her that he needed to know and she wasn't to let up until she found out. I remained firm that I wasn't going to divulge my source, and I kept refusing to tell her.

She, of course, lost her temper and started shouting at me. I continued to calmly prepare dinner and told her that she wouldn't get any information out of me. She then reached for a kitchen knife in the butcher's block and started to threaten me with it! I told her to put it down and that she should leave the house. She refused and stood there defiantly, although she did put the knife away.

"Get out of the house, Amy, if you're going to threaten me!" I said, now raising my voice also.

"Not till you tell me who ratted on Luke!"

"I'm not going to tell you, now get out of the house this minute!"

"No!" She shouted, "I'm not leaving till you tell me!"

"Then I'm calling the police", I answered, going over to the phone. I figured that, since she had threatened me with a knife and was still standing there glaring at me menacingly, saying that I would call the police would make her back off.

Instead, she walked over to a picture on the wall and slammed it as hard as she could with her fist! The picture immediately smashed and fell onto the floor. Blood sprang out of a cut on her hand and all I could say was, "Now look what you've done! Get out of the house immediately, or I'll call the police!"

"No!" she screamed, at which I went to the phone on the wall and dialed 911.

At that point, and I will never forget this, she came up behind me and grabbed me by the throat, attempting to choke me and make me drop the phone. However, at this time in my life, I had been attending the gym regularly and lifting weights. The end result of all this exercising was that I'd become quite strong, whereas Amy hated to go to gym class and had lost weight by taking pills, so she wasn't all that fit. I easily pulled her hands off my throat and dialed the phone again. She then fled upstairs and tried to barricade herself in her room!

The police took their time getting there, I must say. I had to call again and eventually they showed up. The constable was a nice young woman, Cheryl, whom I had met before at Ed's office, and she knew some of

Amy's history of running with delinquent friends and getting drunk in public. She asked me what had happened, and I said Amy had threatened me with a knife and broken a picture on the wall, finishing by attempting to throttle me when I called 911.

"Is that your blood on your neck, or hers?" she asked.

I put my hand up to my neck and it came away with blood on it. I hadn't even made the connection between the cut on Amy's hand and my neck, but it was proof that I wasn't lying.

"Hers," I replied.

The police officer and her partner tried to call Amy down to talk to them, but she replied by calling them the foulest names in the English language. They then went up the stairs and into her room. The sounds of scuffling and multiple swearwords in Amy's voice followed, and then they marched her downstairs in handcuffs. She was fighting and struggling with them, but they managed to get her out to their squad car.

The police officer turned to me before leaving and asked, "Would you like to press charges?"

"No," I replied firmly. "I just wanted her out of the house so she could calm down a little and stop badgering me for the name of the person who told on her boyfriend."

"Well, I'm afraid we have to press charges," she replied. "She'll spend the night in jail and you can come back and get her in the morning."

I was horrified! I didn't realize that my actions would take things so far but, at the same time, I knew that I had had to follow through on my threats to call the police, or lose whatever control I had left over Amy. As soon as I shut the door, I burst into tears, then called Ed on his cellphone to tell him what had happened, instructing him not to react to anything I said so that our German friends wouldn't figure out what was going on at home. Even at that time, I was all about keeping up appearances!

The following period in our lives was extremely stressful. At first, Amy was really mad at me and wouldn't talk to me, but eventually she forgave me (as she always did and was to continue doing for the rest of her life) and things settled down to an uneasy peace in the house.

We were called in to see a probation officer, a nice man whose wife I knew through our playschool board. He was a no-nonsense kind of guy who saw through Amy's blustering and did his best to help us repair our relationship. He told her that, since she was still a minor, she should obey her parents and respect their rules, finish school and stop hanging out with kids who were a bad influence. To give her credit, she mostly listened to what he said (though not ending any of her friendships with the troubled kids), although her emotions continued to be all over the place when things didn't go her way!

She had to go to court, and that was extremely embarrassing for us, as we knew the parents of some of the other juveniles there and all of us were squirming in our seats as our children were called before the judge. When it was Amy's turn, she seemed repentant, but I was angry when the judge said that "her mother pressed charges against her". I didn't – it was the police who did – and I felt betrayed. That was only the very beginning of many years of feeling betrayed by our legal system. Time after time throughout our years of dealing with Amy's behavior, we would be let down by the police and the court system. The police often don't follow through with charges, maybe handicapped by a lack of resources and manpower. As for lawyers and the courts, they seem to pay lip service to justice but, then, when it comes down to actually dealing with miscreants, they choose a course which ends up making the accused look like a victim. This results in lower sentences or dismissal of cases, leaving the families of the victims frustrated and angry.

Amy was given probation and we had to pay a fine for her. When I went with her to pay the clerk (the agreement was that Amy would repay me with wages from the job she was going to look for once the court case was over), the probation officer appeared and asked how it went.

I replied, "She got probation," and hugged her. She hugged me back hard, and I kissed her.

"Look how your mother loves you!" He said to her. "You deserve to grow up and have a daughter just like you!"

We both laughed at that but, in my head, I thanked him silently. I felt that Amy needed proof that I loved her and wasn't just being tough on her because I felt like it. I just wanted what was best for her and for her to turn out to be a respectable member of society. Our immediate family supported her as best we could during those times and made sure that she attended all of her probation meetings.

I did learn, from Amy herself, that she had told her probation officer that her dad was the "nice" parent in the family and that I was the "mean" one. She said that I often treated her unfairly and differently from the other children in the family. This pattern of painting herself as the unloved child in the family persisted throughout her life, and it was often brought up to us in future arguments.

She also told her probation officer that I abused her physically, and that I had got the wooden spoon out of the drawer on the day of our dispute and threatened her with it. He asked her whether she wanted to press charges against me. She claimed that she had told him, "No, I just want this to be over and for our family to move on." I will never know to this day whether this was true or whether it actually happened. I had no recollection of taking the wooden spoon out and threatening her with it. She had become an expert liar and would often tell stories like this, to make herself look like the victim and the other person (usually me!) look bad. It was all part of the problem that was swirling around her and starting to form a pattern in her life, something we were not to understand until much later.

Stephanie

Life continued on, with many ups and downs and visits to the psychologist, which helped somewhat, maybe because Amy and I both felt validated in our feelings. I tried not to react to her rages, but it was often difficult to stay calm. Also, by this time, Stephanie was starting to veer off course. She had, like her sister, grown up into a beautiful young girl. She had always been a good student and did very well in school, although she could be stubborn and rebellious at home. However, by Grade 12, she seemed to have lost interest in her schoolwork and had decided she wanted to be a hairdresser. She later told me that being the sibling of a person like Amy had been very hard on her growing up, and that she felt that all of our attention was directed towards her sister – she had basically been ignored. This translated into some mental health issues for her as she was growing up, but that is another story.

Stephanie enrolled in the cosmetology programme at the high school and did very well, even earning an award. We, however, felt she had the potential to go to university and become a professional of some sort, and we pushed her to pursue that path. She did a second year of grade 12 (usually referred to by students as "grade 13") and finished her apprenticeship as a hairdresser. I encouraged her to enroll in Mount Royal College in Calgary, as her marks weren't good enough for the University of Calgary, and she did so, deciding to take psychology.

However, she had made a friend, Diane, who had come from a broken home and was also in hairdressing. Diane was a "party girl" and encouraged Stephanie to go out to clubs with her, often on weeknights.

Steph would come home, sometimes at one a. m., and I would be furious with her, as she had school (which we were paying for!) the next day. Any time I told her off for coming home late, she would give back as good as she got and the fights were similar to the ones I had with Amy.

Amy, for her part, was fairly compliant at this time and, at one time, confided in me that Stephanie and her friend were doing cocaine when they were out partying. I confronted my elder daughter with this and she denied it vehemently, calling me several choice names as she did it. Eventually, and with Ed's agreement, I told her that she could no longer live at home, as she was an adult and we could not enable her drug habit.

"You simply can't continue to party and do drugs when you're supposed to be in school!" I told her. "And your behaviour is harming our relationship!"

"We have no relationship!" She countered angrily, "I hate you!"

Shortly after that, I found her a room in a house with some friends of her godmother Carla's in Calgary and she moved there, supposedly to continue her studies. Not long afterwards, she met an Italian boy named Roberto (Rob) and they started dating. He had rather a shady past, as we were to find out afterwards, but he swore to us earnestly that he was trying to change his life and be a good support for Steph. She seemed happier at that time, and we tolerated him for her sake.

As it turned out, he was the one who told me one day when I was on the phone with them that she wasn't going to school, and hadn't been as long as they had been dating. After my first reaction of shock and anger at the way we'd been deceived and the amount of money we'd spent on school fees and rent, I asked to speak to Stephanie and demanded to know if this was true. She admitted that it was, and I then told her that she had better get a job and start supporting herself. Well, she did just that, also moving out of the rental place and getting an apartment with Diane. For a while, she seemed to function very well. I believed she was off drugs by then, for Roberto's sake (he had sworn off them, so he said, although we later found out that he continued to smoke pot, which he didn't regard as a "bad habit"). She got herself a job at a salon and started to make money – eventually enough to make payments herself on a cellphone and small car! We were proud of her, although I still wished she had pursued her studies, as I felt she wasn't living up to her potential. That, in fact, was exactly how my mother felt about me – who says we don't become our mothers?

Shortly after that, though, tragedy struck in Steph's young life. Diane had been dating a drug dealer and, after they broke up, she was drinking with a friend at a house in north Calgary. They were both drunk, but decided that they should go and get more beer. The friend was apparently a "speed demon" and Diane, always careless of her own safety, never wore a seatbelt when riding in a car. They sped drunkenly down Bow Trail and were met head-on by another car. Diane was thrown out of the car and died on impact. The friend was seriously injured and broke his spine. At the age of 22, Diane's short life was ended because of negligence and addiction. It was a terrible time for Stephanie. She had really loved her friend and, although a couple of her male classmates had been killed in car accidents after graduating high school, it had never hit so close to home for her! She was devastated.

I will never forget her coming up to our bedroom the next time she came to our house and giving me a big hug when I expressed condolences on her loss of Diane.

She murmured, "I'm so sorry for everything I've put you and Dad through, Mum".

At the time, all I could think of to say was, "It's very hard when you see your kids going down a bad path."

Yes, that's true, but I should have just said, "Thank you", or "Let's go on from here". Although I've learned a lot from my life experiences in the last few years, at the time, I still had a lot of anger in me.

Amy wearing the Marilyn Monroe dress she created herself

Amy Leaves Home

By keeping her nose firmly to the grindstone, helping her with her homework and making her learn her lines when she was in drama productions, we managed to get Amy through high school.

Graduation Day dawned sunny and full of hope, in early June. Amy had continued to pursue her fashion studies, and had decided to make her own grad dress. It was a gorgeous purple shade, which went really well with her blond hair, and had a corset top and full skirt.

Well, she never actually finished making it, and got into a panic when, only a week from Grad, it still wasn't done! My sewing skills weren't up to a dress of that caliber, so I called a friend who had been involved in sewing costumes for the drama department and was a seamstress. She finished the dress beautifully and only charged me $25! As grad was an expensive undertaking and money was still tight, I was grateful for the deal she gave us!

Amy looked stunning in her dress and with her hair beautifully done by her sister. Luke, her date, looking very handsome in his tux, was proud to have her on his arm. Of course, we had the usual drama on the day, with her throwing a temper tantrum over something in the morning and reminding everybody, "This is MY day, not yours!", but we got through it and finally arrived at the ceremony and dinner.

Her peers clapped loudly for her when she crossed the stage, and I felt that all those years of being teased and excluded from the popular groups had maybe come to an end. I was very happy for her on that day and, for a while, things seemed to be going alright with her in her life, although she still continued to fight with us over house rules. She would also often scream at Luke for hours on end on the phone, eventually damaging her voice and being unable to sing the classical music songs she learned in her singing lessons. That was a sad day for her.

She opted for doing Grade 13, like her sister, but decided not to be in the drama production that year, probably because of the loss of her singing voice. Instead, she employed the other talent in which she excelled, which was sewing, and helped the director realize her vision for the costumes in her production of "The Wiz". The director was a fiery young woman, like Amy, and although they loved each other a great deal, they often had yelling matches. I thought the director was very tolerant for allowing Amy to continue in the programme, after dealing with her temper, and I was very grateful to her. At one point, she directed one of our theatre group's plays, in which Amy played a role and, although they had a few disagreements, the play went off successfully and she was pleased with Amy's work.

Amy continued to work part-time while going to school, in a multitude of fast-food jobs, from which she invariably got fired. Her bosses always liked her, but they couldn't put up with her lack of reliability and her general sloppiness on the job. As a result, she rarely had any money and was constantly begging for loans. She had always had problems with managing her money, anyway, and her allowances had burned holes in her pockets when she received them. The only way she had ever been able to buy Christmas presents for her family and friends was if we saved her allowance for her, starting in the beginning of October!

However, after she finished school, she managed to hold on to one of her jobs long enough to qualify for a loan to buy a car. Instead of choosing a small, compact car that wouldn't cost her too much, she chose a second-hand red Jeep Grand Cherokee, as she said she could drive her buddies around in it.

That summer, as she was waiting to take possession of the car, she asked me to give her a ride up to her friend, Lauren's, house. I said I would drive her, and we got into the family van. Half-way up the hill to Lauren's house, by way of making conversation, I asked her,

"Why are you going to Lauren's?"

"She's got a purse she's going to sell me, "she replied.

Outrage immediately surfaced in me. Amy owed money to me and to her siblings, and here she was informing me calmly that her friend was about to sell her a purse! I instantly stopped the car and turned to her.

"You are not going to buy a purse!" I told her sternly. "You owe me money, and your young brother, as well. You should pay off your debts before buying yourself yet another purse!"

I started to turn the car around and she immediately opened the door to get out. However, I wasn't going to let her simply get out of the car and walk up to Lauren's house. There was a lesson to be learned here! I sped up the vehicle, making it impossible for her to get out, and I continued to speed up every time she tried to get out. I was determined not to let her go ahead with a purchase she couldn't afford, when she already owed money. She needed to understand about basic economics if she was going to function in the world and buying items you don't need when you are broke is not a good way to get ahead.

I finally had to stop at a set of lights, and she jumped out of the car and started walking briskly back in the direction of Lauren's house. I knew I had lost the battle, but hoped that I'd made my point.

Later that afternoon, as my mother (a retired physician, who was visiting us at the time) and I were sitting in the backyard, Stephanie's boyfriend Rob showed up at the house.

"I'm the designated driver," he informed me.

"Designated for what?" I asked him.

"To take Amy to the city. Didn't she tell you she's leaving home and moving in with us?" (He and Stephanie were now living together and doing quite well for themselves with two full-time jobs.)

"No!" I replied.

At first, I was upset and felt guilty about my actions that afternoon. However, upon reflection, it seemed for the best. Amy was 19 years old, had her own car, couldn't seem to hold down a job as long as she was living at home, but maybe moving into the city and having to support herself might make her more reliable.

I was sad when she left with Rob, especially as she would barely talk to me, but I felt justified that maybe it was time for her to move on. The constant domestic fights and her staunch refusal to follow any of the rules at home seemed good reasons for her to try life on her own for a while. It was time she grew up!

She didn't actually end up living with Stephanie and Rob. Instead, she moved in with one of Steph's friends, Callum, who had a nice condo and seemed to like her a lot. There was another girl living there, and a liquor store within walking distance, where she found a job. What I didn't know, though, was that Callum had frequent parties, featuring cocaine, and a lot of drugs were used in that apartment, although he didn't actually use them himself (or so I'm told!).

Amy's flight for freedom was just the start of her descent into the world of hard drugs, and it was the beginning of a terrible chapter of her life.

The following Christmas, we went to my brother's in northwest Calgary for dinner. Amy had called and made her peace with us not long after she moved out of our house (which is what she always did after a family fight) and had decided to come back and spend the three days of Christmas Eve through to Boxing Day with us. She and Michael drove up with us, as Stephanie was coming with Rob and meeting us there. After dinner, it started to snow, and there was a serious blizzard by the time that we had to leave for home.

Ed had imbibed a few glasses of wine, so it fell to me to drive home on the highway, which hadn't been ploughed, due to the season. Now, I'm a very nervous driver in bad conditions, though something of a leadfoot on sunny days! I felt I needed my concentration on the highway, so turned the car radio off and requested Amy, who had been talking incessantly on her cellphone, to put the phone away. She refused and ignored me, laughing and shrieking with her friends the whole way home.

As we pulled into the driveway at home, I was in a state of terror from the awful road conditions and fury with Amy for ignoring me. I turned to her and said,

"Amy, don't ever think about coming home for three days again!"

As soon as the words were out of my mouth, I regretted them. I didn't really mean them, but how often do we say things we don't mean because of a stressed out, emotional state? However, it was too late – the hypersensitive Amy perceived this as the worst insult I had ever dealt her and she was furious!

"I'm not staying one more minute in this house!" she raged. "Where are my car keys?"

My regret of my harsh words was instantaneous! How could she be thinking of driving alone back to Calgary in this storm?

"Amy!" I begged. "There's a blizzard out there! You can't leave – you don't have enough experience driving in bad weather!"

"I don't care!" She retorted. "I'm not staying where I'm not wanted! I'm leaving right now!"

"But you'll be killed!" I shouted hysterically.

"I don't care! I hate all of you in this stupid house!"

No amount of begging or coercion could make her change her mind, and she immediately began searching for her keys, spending the next half hour vainly looking for them. Fortunately, I had gone back out to the van to bring in the Christmas presents and spotted the keys lying on the floor of the car. They must have dropped out of her purse when she was talking on the phone.

I scooped them up, hid them in my purse, and then whispered to the now very worried Ed that I had them. He was relieved. She would have to stay at least overnight if she couldn't drive back to Calgary, and maybe she would have calmed down by morning and I could beg forgiveness.

However, she hadn't calmed down by morning at all. She spent most of the rest of the night calling all her friends and trying to get someone (in vain, because of the awful weather) to come and get her. In the morning, she cold-shouldered me, but informed the rest of the family that she planned to leave as soon as she found her keys.

The storm had stopped by then, and the Highways Department had finally ploughed the roads, so I told her that I had found her keys. She then drove herself back to the city, still furious with me.

I know that I had overreacted to her behaviour, but my nerves had been jangling with the constant chatter on the phone and the words escaped me before I thought it through properly. I certainly didn't expect her to want to leave in the middle of a raging blizzard though and, if she had driven in and had an accident, I would never have forgiven myself!

Amy Meets Mark

As always, she phoned us a few days later and asked how we were doing. This was to be a constant pattern with Amy – she would heap scorn on us, and tell us that we were the worst parents (especially me!) in the world then, usually about a week later, she would phone and tell us how much she missed us. It was the one thing that kept our relationship going and prevented us from being estranged. I was always afraid to make the first move, for fear of heaping more venom on myself if she wasn't ready to make up. In those days, I attributed it to her huge, generous heart and that did have a lot to do with it, but the need to keep in contact with us was often very puzzling, given the anger she had shown only a few days before.

Amy had broken up with Luke some time after graduation, saying that he had scarred her mentally for life and that she could never go out with him again. Although they remained friends (she, in fact, remained friends with all of her boyfriends except one), she had nothing good to say about him in those days. Unknown to us, she had, at one time, become pregnant and, since he was already a father to one child born out of wedlock, he had become extremely upset with her. She had got information from a friend and arranged an abortion for herself at a clinic in Calgary. (At the time, she told me that she was "holding the hand" of a girlfriend while the friend had the procedure – her ability to look me in the eye and lie had become masterful, and I fell for every word!) However, after that, things were never quite the same between her and Luke. He is, in fact, a nice man – he was just going through the usual teenage rebellion and had been traumatized by having a child very young and not being able to support that child. The thought of going through that again terrified him! He has, however, grown up to be a successful father of two, and we still communicate with him sometimes.

Amy had been fired from the liquor store and had started to work at a call centre, doing telemarketing. There she had met a young man named Mark and they began dating, very soon falling in love. After losing her job at the liquor store, she failed to pay her rent to Callum and he evicted her. A friend of hers from private school, Frances, a deeply troubled young woman who had been into drinking and drugs for many years and who had also had a child out of wedlock, had hooked up with Amy again while she lived at Callum's. The two of them had made his life very difficult with their partying and drug use at his house. Amy's car was also crashed in an accident involving T-boning another vehicle and ended up being written off. She always claimed that Frances was driving it, without her permission, but I never knew if this was true as Amy always covered her tracks.

As soon as Callum evicted her, she went to live with Mark. At first, everything was rosy and she was very happy there. I visited her there one day and met him. He was a shy young man who had a good, steady job and shared his apartment with a roommate.

It wasn't very long before there was trouble in paradise, though. First of all, Amy got fired from the call centre. She used to have fun with her otherwise boring job and would put on different accents to talk to the potential customers, much to the chagrin of her supervisor! She also had great difficulty getting up in the morning (which was a lifelong problem for her) and would often be late for work. The management finally had had enough of that, and she was given her walking papers.

After that, she failed to look for work. She continued to stay at Mark's apartment, expecting him to support her, claiming that she was a "house-wife" and that she would clean the place for him and his roommate. Well, I went there a couple of times, and the place was in the same state of disarray that her room had been in when she lived at home! His room-mate became irate at the freeloader who was staying with them and not contributing to the rent, and many angry fights followed.

Mark tried to work things out with her, but he was continually taken aback by the extremes of her anger and the way that she would rail at him for everything, claiming that he was the cause of all of her problems in the world. This would be a constant factor in any disagreements with Amy, and it was also something that we had experienced. We felt that it was her own lack of a sense of consequence to her actions, and that she should own up to her own role in the problems in her life.

After one particularly nasty fight, they arrived on our doorstep one night, and I urged him to take her to the Rockyview Psychiatric Ward. The behaviour that he had described to me was very scary, and she had apparently threatened suicide. He did take her there, but she was released the next morning. The staff felt that the suicide was just an empty threat and that she was safe in Mark's care. It wasn't the first time she was to threaten to kill herself.

Time marched on, and by now we had other problems. Stephanie, who had at one time broken up with Rob, had now become engaged to him. They had missed each other greatly after the breakup, and he had asked her to come up and visit him at his job up north. One weekend, she did that, they reconciled and got engaged. Then, about two months later, she told us that she was pregnant.

I was devastated! Stephanie was only 22, I wasn't sure that Rob would be a good father and supporter of a family (he also was continuously fired from jobs, due to his cocky attitude and persistent habit of pot-smoking), and I had always felt that she should go back to university and pursue a professional career. However, she decided to become a mom and they set a wedding date of September 10, 2005, nine months after their baby was born. Amy was equally upset by Stephanie's desire to become a wife and mother, as she felt she wasn't ready for it, but she supported her as best she could. (Little did I know it, but Amy had briefly become a mother also, with Mark, and had terminated the pregnancy in the early stages.)

Stephanie gave birth to a beautiful baby boy, named Luiciano on January 29th of 2005 and she and Rob settled into parenting. At least, he continued to work one job after another and to support the family, after a fashion. They never had any money and, whatever money they did have, he spent on pot and driving his friends around in their vehicle. The fact that Stephanie had worked steadily as a hairdresser after leaving Mount Royal and had qualified for maternity benefits was the only thing that kept them going. We were thrilled with our little grandson, and did our best to help them out wherever we could. Amy and Michael also doted on their little nephew. Amy had always professed to dislike children, and to not want to have any. It was typical of her narcissism that she didn't want children – in fact, she had once stated that it was because "they took the attention away from me"! But she loved little Luc, and indeed I always saw her to be very sweet and kind towards little children.

Amy (left) with Stephanie at her wedding, Sept. 2005

Keith Comes Into Amy's Life

Meanwhile, Amy's relationship with Mark was faltering seriously and, by the time that Stephanie's wedding rolled around, he had thrown all of her belongings onto the lawn of his apartment building and told her he never wanted to see her again. She informed us that he was mentally ill, and that they were finished forever. However, she followed her usual pattern of phoning him a few days later and making up with him. They never got back together, but remained friends, and he often rescued her from some of the dire situations she got herself into later on with future boyfriends (and even from us, at one time, when we told her that she could no longer live with us, due to her risky lifestyle).

The day of Stephanie's wedding dawned cold and blustery, with driving rain lasting for the whole day. Poor Stephanie had planned an outdoor wedding, and was bitterly disappointed with the way things turned out. Her perfect, outdoor wedding remained just a dream and she had to settle for an indoor celebration. Thanks to our friend, Carla, though, it was beautiful. Carla is very talented in the areas of decorating and interior design.

Amy was her maid of honour and, in an effort to make sure that Amy got to the wedding on time (Amy's tardiness, which had made itself evident in her teen years, had become worse as she got older and was the source of many a family joke), Stephanie had insisted that Amy stay overnight with her. Their school chum, Krista, was the other bridesmaid, and was currently dating the drug dealer ex-boyfriend of Stephanie's late friend, Diane. When I arrived at the wedding venue and went to see the girls, they all looked stunningly beautiful, happy and excited about the wedding. I was a proud mum that day, and Ed was a proud father of the bride. Also, our fears that everyone would be late because of Amy's inability to arrive on time were groundless!

The wedding went off without a hitch (except for the weather), and Amy ended up dancing all night with the best man. She dated him briefly for a while but that, like most of her relationships, didn't last.

We didn't know it at the time, but someone much more sinister had come into her life. When she was thrown out of Mark's apartment, she asked her friend, Frances, where she could go. Frances gave her the name of a man, saying "This guy can probably help you out". At the time,

I thought he was a Good Samaritan who helped young girls find work and places to live. But it wasn't very long afterwards that we found out that he was a drug dealer with a long criminal record, who introduced Amy to a life of hard drugs and crime. It was also around this time of her life that she started to call herself "Amijane Marshall". I never knew whether it was an attempt to distance herself from us, or just an alias to protect her real identity when she embarked on a life of crime. I just found out recently that the "Amijane" was for "Mary Jane", the street name for marijuana, and the surname Marshall was for one of her high school "skid" friends, who had died at a young age.

She fell madly in love with Keith, and it wasn't long before she was dating him. She moved in with him and they embarked on a life of crime together. His modus operandi, and favourite form of miscreant behaviour, was to steal Ford 350 trucks, drive them for a while, then sell the parts to "chop shops". He also stole computers, TVs, furniture and anything else that took his fancy. Amy continued to fail at finding lasting work (she worked for three days at a clothing store, as the "Day Supervisor", but was fired when she stole the $600 night deposit that she was supposed to be taking to the bank!). He taught her how to break and enter, and she did actually break into our house through the basement windows at one time. Luckily, I was alerted by the neighbours and soon figured out that it was she and Keith.

We were on holiday in B. C. and Amy broke in, subsequently "entertaining" Keith and his sister, Jenna, and her boyfriend, Matt. Apparently, Stephanie had decided to drop by the house one day with Rob and the baby, and Rob had commented that the white S.U.V. on the driveway looked like a "drug dealer's vehicle". A few days after they left, Ed noticed that the camera which had belonged to our theatre company and which had been left out on a counter (we weren't expecting anyone to be at our house while we were away) had gone missing. After that incident, Ed had bars installed on the basement windows so that break-ins could not happen again!

But the worst form of criminal behaviour that Keith taught Amy was identity theft. They would search through dumpsters for documents that had been thrown away, or steal purses and wallets, then use the information that they found to steal money from people's credit cards or to use their social insurance cards to gain access to their records. He also introduced her to crystal meth, which was an addiction that she had for the rest of her life.

This was all very scary, but even worse was the physical abuse that was predominant in their relationship. He would beat her whenever they had a fight and, at one time, even tried to run her over with one of his stolen Ford 350 trucks! I know that she wasn't innocent of starting the fights, and her way of losing her temper and then goading the other person with false accusations and melodramatic threats was very difficult to deal with, but he was also emotionally unstable, and followed his abusive father's example of beating anyone who locked horns with him.

His sister, Jenna, was also abusive. At one time, Keith had apparently gone on a "business trip" (probably to pick up some drugs from another province) and he had left Amy in the house with Jenna and Matt, who were staying with them at the time. Amy later told me that she had had an argument with Jenna over something, which had then resulted in the pair of them tying her up in the basement and keeping her down there for three days, beating her periodically! We never found out why, or if it was even true, but it was extremely shocking. There's a possibility that Amy had stolen something from Jenna and that they had locked her up until she told them where it was, but that doesn't excuse the savage behaviour.

Keith was equally cruel. I remember Amy calling me once when I was in a grocery store, sobbing that he was beating her relentlessly. She said that they were at an acreage out in the country (they moved constantly from one place to another, dependent on criminal "friends" who could put them up for a day or two) and begging me to come and rescue her. She suddenly hung up, and I tried to call her back. She wouldn't pick up, and texting elicited no response either. I worried and fretted all the way home, then told Ed about it as soon as I arrived. I was afraid that Keith would murder her! Ed had a patient in the RCMP, and we asked for his help in tracking Amy down and seeing if she was still alive.

He did so, and called a couple of days later to say that Amy and Keith were back in Calgary, and that she was fine. He also said that he had talked to Keith's mother, who lived in Calgary as well, and she had assured him that her son wouldn't kill anybody.

Later that day, I got a furious call from Amy. "What were you thinking?" she yelled at me on the phone. "How dare you call the cops on Keith? Don't you know he could go to jail if they check his warrants?"

I didn't care about that – actually, I hoped that they would take him to jail, so that he would lose his hold on our daughter and she would be able to free herself of the criminal lifestyle she had adopted while she was with him.

Amy 2007

Amy Comes Home Again

Amy had made some attempts to stop her drug habit, which was ingesting or smoking crystal meth. She had said that she liked the drug because it kept her skinny, and she no longer had to worry about watching her weight. However, on the few occasions that we saw her, she was looking dangerously thin – her collarbones jutting out and her face skeletal. She was also frequently dirty and dressed in torn and messy clothes. She had a habit of smearing herself with fake tanning lotion, but would never put it on properly, and it would be streaked all over her face and arms, furthering the impression of being dirty and unkempt. Her hair was also always a mess, sometimes with hair extensions in it that were not clipped in properly. Her fashion style had deteriorated hugely over the years, although this had started in high school, when she affected the low-slung pants and broken footwear of the skids.

In an attempt to free herself of her drug habit, she had asked Keith to take her to Renfrew, the detox centre for drug addicts in Calgary. Apparently, she weighed less than 90 lbs when she went there, and was accepted immediately. However, her heart wasn't really in her recovery, and she resumed her habit as soon as she came out.

During the summer of 2007, she had a falling out with Keith, worse than most – it may have been the time that he tried to run her over with his truck. She made up her mind to leave him and called us, requesting to come back home. This was the first of three attempts to come home and try to turn her life around.

I told her, "Yes, you can come back, if you promise to get a job and stay clean. You also have to help with household chores and pay rent once you're earning a paycheque."

She promised me faithfully that she would and she moved back in just a few days later. My widowed mum was staying with us at the time, and Amy was happy about that, as she had often professed that my mum was her "favourite grandparent". (We had once foolishly enlisted Ed's parents' help when both Stephanie and Amy were hanging around with the skids during high school and blatantly ignoring our house rules. I thought that our girls would be more willing to listen to their grandparents than to us, whom they no longer respected. How wrong I was. The scene that ensued was very ugly. Amy did most of the arguing and, at one point, my mother-in-law told her that she was crazy. It certainly must have seemed that way to her! Stephanie was willing to forgive her grandma and grandpa soon after for their part in the telling-off that the two girls got; but Amy took much longer to get over it, and actually told people for many years that her paternal grandparents "hated" her! Of course, they didn't at all, and were always very loving grandparents to our kids.)

Well, as was to continue to be a pattern later on, Amy came home and made no effort whatsoever to find a job. Her room soon deteriorated into a horrible mess, with clothing, belongings and food on the floor, and she actually decided to punch holes in the walls, from which to hang ornate bedcurtains and scary-looking artwork, which reflected her gothic tastes in art and fashion. Her bedroom looked like a nineteenth century whore's boudoir, with frightening modern art on the walls! She also refused to do chores or help with the cooking of meals, which she should have done, as Ed and I were both still working.

Any attempt at urging her to clean her room or put away her dishes would be met with screaming resentment. In fact, one day, when I tried to get her out of bed to go to a job interview, she, furious at being woken up, started screaming at me,

"You're the worst mother in the world! I should hang myself for having you for a mother!" She then followed this up with calling me the worst names that she could think of, and telling me where to go.

I should have realized that this was not normal behaviour, but I put it down to withdrawal from drug use, and that she was needing her next "fix". I wasn't convinced that she'd given up her habit and told her one day that I felt she was still using drugs. I thought that maybe this would explain her extremes of behaviour. She responded by sitting down, with tears in her eyes, and saying plaintively,

"Mum, you don't realize how much you hurt me when you say that I'm doing drugs. It's really hard for me to hear that!"

Looking back, I know that this was just a smokescreen for the fact that she was still doing drugs, and it was also an indication of the state of her mental health. We now know that addiction is a mental illness but, back then, we just put her behaviour down to an inability to kick her bad habit, and to curb her over-the-top temper.

Apparently, she and my mum sat down for a little talk over a cup of tea not long after this, and she confessed to my mum how she and Keith had been supporting themselves when they were together. She seemed almost proud of the way they were able to steal people's identities and credit cards, telling Mum it was just a matter of "doing the math". Mum responded,

"But, Amy, don't you realize that you're hurting people with your actions and that it's against the law?"

Amy didn't seem to care, and in fact was quite self-congratulatory about the whole thing. My mum commented at the time that she felt Amy had sociopathic tendencies. I couldn't help but agree with her, given the behaviours we had witnessed in the last few years. However, she wrote my mum a beautiful letter not long after, apologizing for her bouts of temper and screaming obscenities during Mum's stay.

Here is the letter Amy wrote to her:

Aug 14/07

"Dear Bucky," (this was the name that Stephanie had given my mother when she was only 18 months old. My mum decided that she would rather be called "Bucky" than "Grandma", and all my kids called her that afterwards!). "Hi, I am composing this letter to you because I sometimes am better with my words on paper than verbally, plus you are able to keep this and read it whenever you feel, to remind you that I'm not just the worst person/daughter/granddaughter on the planet.

"I would like to start by offering you my sincerest apologies for my out of line behavior during your stay. I wish that it wasn't such a (sic) unfortunate coincidence, your stay and my life meltdown, because I know how uncomfortable it can be for a person when there's a crazy rambling time bomb in the house. There is no excuse for my behavior and outbursts, other than I am not stable enough to hold a glass on my head, let alone deal with and accept wich (sic) is occurring in my life. Thank you for being still even willing to talk to me and be in the same house as me. I can hardly stand myself lately which is why I keep so alone. No one needs a mad killer like me around. I have enjoyed very much though the talks we have had and I am so glad you are here visiting and that I actually was able to see you this time! I hope very much so that you don't take my bitchiness and irritability personally, because it is not at all that I am being mean or rude to anyone and any particular reason. It's because I can't even control my emotions and anger seems to come easier to me than my own language. I'm just not happy with anywhere in my life. I am sorry for taking it out on you and Mum and everyone, for that matter. None of you deserve to be spazzed

at the way I have been treating everyone. I am very sorry. Please don't hate me. I hope you do understand and forgive me, because this isn't me and I do love all of you very much. I know that I am here for help, not force. Thank you for wanting to be a part in my recovery. I am sorry and I do love you and thank and enjoy your visit and time u have spent with me.

Love,

Ami-Jane"

It was such a lovely letter. My mum was very touched by it, and did in fact keep it, sending me a copy of it after we lost Amy. We have kept it in a special memorabilia jar that we have for Amy, and I bring it out from time to time, to remind me of the sweetness and insight Amy so often showed. It always brings me to tears! It also was an indication that Amy was very much aware of the aberrations in her behaviour and their affect on other people, especially loved ones.

In spite of the beautiful letter and chat with my mum, Amy's behaviour that summer continued to deteriorate. After Mum left, more horrible screaming matches occurred and a continuation of Amy's erratic and inflammable temper. We finally insisted that she go to a rehab facility, as we were sure that it was drugs that were fuelling her moods. Little did we know it then, but the drug use was only a symptom of what was really going on.

We were told that she couldn't go to rehab without doing a week of detox first and, although we tried to get her into Renfrew, it was full, and they could see that she had us to take care of her, so she was refused. Ed then found a place in Fort Macleod, a town south of Okotoks, that could take her and, although full, they often had "no shows" and they suggested that he bring her there and leave her for the day. She could then be admitted during the evening.

One Sunday morning, he drove her to Fort Macleod. I stayed in bed until after they left, as I really didn't want to face her and a possible fight about going to detox. By insisting that she seek treatment, I had become the enemy by now, and could do nothing right in Amy's estimation.

Ed called me after they arrived there. He said that Amy had decided that she didn't want to go to rehab, after all. He insisted that she stay in the car, and was able to keep her there until they reached the detox facility. When they arrived, they were informed (as he knew) that she would have to wait around until the evening, and then be admitted if there were any no-shows.

Furious, Amy yelled at her father, "This is bull****!!" she screamed. "I'm NOT going to detox and I'm NOT going to hang around here all day!"

Ed had always been a peacemaker. Not wanting to wait around in Fort Macleod all day with a belligerent and "jonesing" girl, he drove her first to the RCMP, as he knew that she and Keith had outstanding warrants against them, and he hoped they might take Amy to their jail and then send her back to Calgary for court. The RCMP officer looked her up on CPIC, and then announced that it was "out of his jurisdiction". Yet another letdown from our legal system! We hadn't experienced enough letdowns yet to become jaded, but that would eventually set in.

Ed then drove her to a local café and gave her $40.

"You can either stay here all day and buy yourself food with this money, then go to the Detox Centre tonight, or you can buy yourself a Greyhound ticket back to Calgary. Your choice," he told her.

Well, addicts have to want to help themselves. Nobody else can force them to seek recovery. It had been our idea to take her to detox, not hers so, needless to say, Ed saw her walking towards the Greyhound station as he drove away. Amy later told me that Keith had texted her during the drive to Fort Macleod, begging her to come back and start a new life with him.

Note: Jonesing refers to an addict's need for the drug of their choice.

Stephanie Becomes A Single Mom

During the course of her 10 month marriage to Rob, Stephanie had become pregnant with a second baby. Ed and I were very worried about Rob's ability to support one child, let alone two, and Amy had been upset with her for getting pregnant yet again. Stephanie, however, seemed very happy with the prospect of becoming a mother again in November.

Money continued to be an issue for them and, because they could hardly ever afford to pay their rent (Rob spent most of her maternity benefits as soon as they were received), they decided to move up to Leduc to live with Rob's father and stepmother. Stephanie wasn't happy about the move, which would take her away from her family, friends and support system, but she went with Rob, willing to give it a chance.

It was a disaster! They lived in the basement of the father-in-law's house and, although the stepmother was kind to them, Rob continued to lose jobs and the father-in-law started to demand rent from them.

Then Stephanie phoned us in mid-June to say that she could no longer feel the baby moving, and was scheduled for an ultrasound to check whether everything was all right. The following Sunday was Father's Day, and I was planning on having our whole family over for a barbecue, which was the family's traditional way of spending Father's Day.

On the Saturday, we received a tearful phone call from Stephanie to say that the baby had died and that they were going to have to induce labour to remove the fetus the next day. Heartbroken for my poor daughter, I asked her if she wanted me to come and be with her for the procedure and she replied that she did.

It was a very sad time for all of us. The doctors said that the baby had been a girl, and we all cried in the hospital room when she was delivered (including the very compassionate nurses). They asked me whether I wanted to see her, and I said that I did, but advised Stephanie to just keep her thoughts of how the baby had looked before she died. A 20-week fetus doesn't really look like a normal baby, and I didn't want her to have bad memories afterwards. I think Stephanie regrets to this day that she didn't see and hold her tiny offspring. Perhaps I made the wrong decision in suggesting that she not see the baby, but I guess that we all act on our best beliefs at the time.

A couple of days later, Rob suggested that Steph and Luc return to Okotoks with me, rather than going home, to have a little "holiday" and get over the horror of the stillbirth. They agreed that they would, and we all drove back from Leduc that day. She returned a few days later, with the promise to come back for the July long weekend.

On July 1st, Stephanie came back to Okotoks and she was furious with Rob! She said that he had been up north working and that she had made some appointments in Calgary to do haircuts and perms for friends of hers. She had a time deadline and, when he still hadn't returned from work to accompany her to Calgary, she left without him. He called her many times, begging her to wait for him, but she didn't want to let down her friends, and so refused. He was very angry with her, and they hung up from their phone calls on bad terms.

The next day, he called her and told her that he was driving to Okotoks and wanted her to go out for "coffee" with him. His father was bringing him from Leduc, and then they planned to return immediately up north. It all seemed very strange, but we agreed to take care of Luc while she went for the coffee date.

When she returned, she had a face like thunder and informed us that Rob had just "broken up" with her and wanted to end their short-lived marriage! We were all absolutely devastated – how could he leave her only two weeks after she had lost their stillborn baby? How could any man be so heartless as to do that?

Rob claimed that Stephanie, who had gradually lost patience with him for failing to support their family and spending all of their money on pot-smoking and driving friends around, had "scarred" him with the things she had said to him! He said he couldn't continue living like that and so wanted the marriage to end.

The truth was that he had found another girl, Toni, and was planning to replace Stephanie with her. He dated her for another year, then broke up with her and started seeing yet another girl, Beatrice. He and Beatrice subsequently had two little girls then, over the course of the next four years, he was unfaithful to her with her cousin, and she kicked him out. He had a pattern of constant philandering, and this has never changed. His father, who never actually raised him and didn't even meet him until he was 14, was exactly the same. The power of genetics!

Well, Stephanie was well rid of him. She came back to live with us, after moving from Leduc, and got herself a job as the manager of the hair salon in the Bay in a nearby mall. She found a daycare in Calgary for Luc while she was at work, and they lived with us until January of the next year. She had meanwhile put her name on the list for Subsidized Housing in Calgary, but was told that the waiting list was long.

We weren't comfortable with her driving on the highway during the winter, and I had visions of her skidding off the road with baby Luc in the back of the car. At that time, my in-laws always went to Arizona for the winter and had often lamented not being able to find anyone reliable to look after their house while they were gone. I suggested Stephanie and, since the Bay was literally only 5 minutes' walk from their house, it seemed like the ideal situation. She moved into their house that January and, literally one week after they returned from Arizona, she got a call from Assisted Housing to say that they had a 2-bedroom apartment available in the West Hills area of Calgary and she could move in right away.

Not long after that, frustrated with standing on her feet all day and with fussy women who didn't like your work and came back to get their hair done again for free, she decided to give up hairdressing and go back to school.

Stephanie has worked extremely hard to get where she is today. She went to Southern Alberta Institute of Technlogy to upgrade her grade 12 grades (which, you may remember, hadn't been all that stellar) and then was accepted into the University of Calgary psychology programme. She had always enjoyed psychology at Mount Royal and wanted to pursue a career in it, to help troubled people figure out what was ailing them. Possibly having a sister with Amy's problems prompted her, but she also had some issues of her own which she has been contending with ever since.

In spite of being a single mother and working to support herself and Luc during the school year and summer vacations (and with no financial help from Rob), she received a first-class honours B. Sc. degree in psychology, and is now working on a second degree in kinesiology, with a view to helping women with eating disorders through holistic means. She still does hair for family members and friends once in a while, and being a single mother has been a big struggle for her, but she has done really well, and we're proud of her.

Amy Breaks Up With Keith

Amy had started another new life with Keith, using crystal meth and being beaten by him whenever they had a fight. She occasionally came home for family dinners, but we saw less and less of her. She rarely talked about the abuse, and it was really only after they broke up that we learned how bad it was.

At one point, we offered to pay for her to go to school for massage therapy, in which she had expressed an interest on several occasions. We said that we would pay her rent while she was in school, so she took us up on our offer. However, we soon got a call from the president of the college to say that Amy was only attending class sporadically. Upon further questioning of her, she replied that Keith had developed pneumonia and that she had had to stay home to take care of him.

I confided in the gentleman that I believed it was more likely drug use that kept her away from school, and he told me that his own daughter had had issues with drugs and a bad boyfriend. Thankfully, she had broken up with the boyfriend and come back home to them. She was now clean and helping him with the administration of the school. If only our daughter had had a success story like that! After about two months of spotty attendance, and then no attendance at all, the president phoned me again and said that Amy no longer had enough hours to complete the course and would have to leave.

This was not the only occasion of lack of continuation when it came to further education for our wayward daughter!

That year, she didn't even come home for Christmas – we had to drop off her presents to the house she was living in. It was a bungalow in Bridgeland, a residential area in Calgary, which had bars on the windows and a front door which was barricaded with strong beams. She and Keith claimed that it was "to keep people from breaking in and stealing things". Upon reflection, I think it was to prevent the police from coming in when they found one of the miscreants who lived there! They were eating a turkey dinner which Frances, who had resurfaced, claimed to have cooked for them. She had probably just stolen it from her mother, or from the person with whom she had been living at the time!

And, on the subject of stealing, not long after Amy went back to Keith that fall, we realized that a coin collection of Ed's had gone missing and that there were huge charges on several of our credit cards! Some membership funds, belonging to our theatre group, had also gone missing, although Amy blamed that on a friend of Keith's whom she had briefly entertained at our house while she was staying with us. We figured we knew who was responsible for the thefts, but Amy always denied them and claimed innocence when she was questioned about them. To our shame, we probably should have pressed charges against her, but we didn't. We let the credit card companies know what was going on and told them it was probably our daughter, but we stopped shy of informing the police, in an effort to maintain some sort of relationship with her. It was a very stressful time for all of us as a family, especially with the difficulties that Stephanie was experiencing with her marriage breaking up.

The following spring, Amy told us that she had attempted suicide. Keith had disappeared for a few days, and she soon found out that he had been staying with another girl. We didn't know much about what exactly happened, but apparently, one of her girlfriends found her and phoned Keith to come home and drive her to the hospital. He must have still had a few shreds of affection for her, as he did return home and took her to Emergency immediately. She had overdosed, but was going to be all right. We didn't find out on which drug she had overdosed, but it may have been crystal meth, or even heroin. She didn't tell us about it until several weeks later but, by then, her relationship with him was in tatters.

Shortly after that, she called us to say that the police had finally caught up to him, because of yet another truck theft, and that he was in jail. She had been kicked out of the apartment where she had been staying, as the landlord felt no obligation to keep her. She had shoplifted to provide herself with clothes and food and been arrested by the police. Eventually released on bail, she had failed to appear in court.

On May 26th, our entire family was leaving a restaurant after celebrating my mother-in-law's 80th birthday. Stephanie had left a few minutes earlier with little Luc and they were on their way home to her new boyfriend, Mike. All of a sudden, my cellphone rang. It was Stephanie – she had been stopped by the police as they drove home and had been arrested for failure to appear in court on shoplifting and counterfeit charges.

In shock, I told the family what had happened, adding "It was Amy who did that, not Stephanie!!"

When we arrived at the scene, Stephanie was sitting in the back of the police cruiser, and had called Mike to come and pick up Luc. Ed said that he would drive Lukey back in her car to her apartment, to be looked after by Mike, and she would have to go to the police station with the officers. We assured them repeatedly that it wasn't our elder daughter who had done the shoplifting and passing of counterfeit money, but the younger one, who had been living a criminal life for the last two years. Obviously, she had given her sister's name when she was arrested and the warrants for failing to appear in court were in Stephanie's name!

Poor Stephanie had to go downtown and share a jail cell with prostitutes before the police were finally satisfied that it was not she who had committed the crime. She was released at about three in the morning, and it was a very long time before she forgave her sister for her perfidy. She later told me that, once during her teen years, she had been stopped by a bylaw officer who said that he knew her and had encountered her many times when she was younger. She replied that she didn't know him, and the penny finally dropped that Amy had been giving Stephanie's name to officers of the law for many years whenever she got in trouble!

It was a sign to me that Amy was a serious sociopath, and that she didn't even hesitate to finger her sister in order to get herself out of trouble. In fact, later on, Stephanie asked Amy why she had called herself Stephanie when she was questioned as to her identity. She had replied, "Well, what was I supposed to do?"

I was sure that the drugs had somehow altered her brain and that that was the reason that she had happily indulged in a life of crime, had no qualms of conscience and was even proud of it. Everything I had read about addicts seemed to apply to Amy, especially the behavior of stealing and lying to others, including their families and friends.

Amy in 2008

The Revolving Door

It was around this time that I, and possibly Ed too, experienced a serious 'disconnect' in our feelings and attitudes about everything that was going on in our lives and, in particular, with our relationship with Amy. We deeply loved our daughter, and I felt that we could somehow steer her straight if only we could control every aspect of her life. A lot of the things she had done were morally wrong and illegal. We knew it and, although we felt in our hearts that they were wrong, we felt powerless to turn our backs on her and leave her to the consequences of her actions. To this day, I've never been able to reconcile to myself that I was only trying to protect her – maybe I was just enabling her, but would we have lost her a lot sooner, if we hadn't? This question continually bothered me, and I still haven't found a satisfactory answer to it for myself, to this day.

When she called in early summer and begged us to let her come home again and live with us, I said yes. She had nowhere else to go, and was basically living on friends' couches, moving around every few days. She had tried to go to the various women's shelters, but they were full and had refused her because she didn't have children. Her pride and some vestige of snobbery left over from her childhood had her convinced that she was "too good" for the homeless shelter, and that home was the only place where she could function.

We agreed, with conditions. She had to clean up her drug habit and turn herself in to the police for the shoplifting, failure to appear, and for her impersonation of Stephanie. She agreed, and Ed went and brought her back to our home. He had just finally got our garage cleaned out from all the theatre props we had been storing in it and was able to park his vehicle for one night, and then all of her stuff (which had been stored at a friend's) was moved into it the very next day!

However, once she was back at home, we tried in vain to hold her to her promise and convince her to give herself up to the police. Ed even phoned them and informed them that she was staying with us and that they could come and get her, but they never came. (Another strike against the legal system!) I knew that she was guilty and that she had deeply hurt her sister, but I still let her stay with us, against my better judgment. A part of me was certain that I could rescue this child, and that it was my duty to her to try to reform her and turn her into a decent citizen, in spite of everything that had gone on. Another thing that held me back from forcing her to go to the police was that I felt, given her tempestuous nature and easily-provoked anger, that she would have been killed if she had gone to jail.

I don't think Stephanie forgave me until recently. She felt deeply let down by her parents for not turning their backs on the sister who had injured her so deeply. My friend, Carla, her Godmother, was also disappointed with me, but nothing would deter me from trying to "fix" my broken child. I don't know if it was my arrogance in believing that I could change anything, or whether it was just desperation to somehow try to salvage this person who had gone so terribly wrong. Like many other parents of addicts, I really believed that there was just one more thing I needed to do which would put my child back on the straight and narrow path and lead her to give up her terrible habit forever. I hope Stephanie now understands where we were coming from, even though she may still feel that we chose Amy's welfare over her reputation and dignity.

So, Amy came home, and this time things were very different from the last time. Perhaps because she no longer had access to the hard drugs (I'm not sure crystal meth was available in Okotoks at that time) or to the toxic boyfriend, but she did actually fit back in to family life with Ed and me. Her bedroom was once again in the basement and, although it was never tidy, she maintained the whole bottom floor as her "little apartment" and I kept myself from censuring her about its state of cleanliness by not going down there! She also applied for a job, and got it, at the local tattoo parlour that had recently opened up in downtown Okotoks. The gentleman who ran it, Sam, seemed to genuinely like her, and she loved her work. She was the receptionist, and booked the appointments for the tattoo artists. Thanks to her work there, she acquired a tattoo on one of her legs of a doll with a knife through its heart. I thought it was sinister, but she explained that it embodied her feelings about men and the way that they mishandle young girls' hearts. It was supposed to represent her feelings towards Keith, and was the first of several tattoos that demonstrated Amy's lifelong fascination with body art.

Her work was within walking distance in the summer and fall, and I often drove her there during the winter months. She actually paid us some rent on a couple of occasions and, since she was happy with her new life, we had no fights. The fact that I didn't bug her about cleaning her room, and that she did once in a while lend a hand with dishes (and even cooked a meal once when Ed and I were working late!) made for a pleasant atmosphere of cooperation between the three of us. She exhibited a "reasonableness" during this period of her life that we were never to see again, and we thought it was because she was off the drugs. She even joined the theatre group again and helped out with some of the productions, but mostly by doing makeup and hair, not acting.

That Christmas, she wrote us a beautiful letter, which was to be our Christmas present, as she never had any money to spend on gifts (her spendthrift ways continued to follow her!).

This is the text of her letter:

"Dear Daddy & Mummie" (she had started calling us by these childhood names once again, and was to do so for the rest of her life),

"I know this probably seems like a weak gift idea, but being as I am retarded and incomeless (with no work), I can't afford material gifts . . . so I'm going to give you guys the best gift I can see fit, that is my words, warped thoughts on paper, but most importantly, my upmost (sic) sincere written gratitude and thanx for the life you stand by so lovingly and shockingly supportive, as well so loyally.

"I sometimes don't take notice of the s*** you guys do for me, after the hell and B.S. I plowed on you since day one, any sane person would have given up even trying. Lol! But we are "Sandses" and it does take a lot to let us give up, I think. But it really keeps me going to know that I have parents like you guys. On the days when I would rather throw myself into the traffic, just one phone call and I know life will pull through. I'm sure it seems as tho I just use and abuse and manipulate to have a free ride and get wut (sic) I want, but honestly in recent months I've really grown to worship the two of you . . . Thank you for putting up with my B.S., and still having faith in me as a person. I love that very slowly I am visibly being shown trust again. I don't feel like such a scumbag in your home any more.

"Yes, I know the trip to rehab has taken SO much longer than anticipated and prayed for, but I have never felt as tho there was a reason for me to fix my goofiness. Wot a selfish, ignorant, self-centred world I had been living in, but I should be ashamed . . . well, I really am, very much so.

"You guys gave me life on a silver platter, and of course like a greedy, over-privileged punk, I took no notice or glanced at the hurt, pain and insult, better yet disrespect, that I gave back in return. I wish then that I knew or acknowledged that I probably have near the best set of parents.

"Wut kind of retard gets mad because their parents clean out their paraphernalia and criming aids? or insist that they go to court? Obviously one who can't determine the difference between right and wrong . . . if I could punch myself in the face for every time I throw in your faces the good you guys were trying to and are still doing for me . . . s***, I'd be near a pulp. Lol!

"I hope that my words here are being taken for wut it's worth, I know it's probably a little, a little too late, but I promise you guys I'm not a lost cause. I won't let you guys down anymore. The day when you can actually be proud . . . well, at least not hesitant . . to tell people about me that ask you guys is so close that I can taste it. I just the other day came to realize I'm an adult, it's time to start being one.

"I do want this change, I am so grateful and thankful you are here with me seeing it thru. Words can't express . . . so I guess my future actions had better prove it, hey?

"I want to be the child you guys put into for me and I am determined to.

"Thank you for your faith, belief, love and hope in me. Thank you so much. I love you guys with all my heart.

"THANK YOU! Don't give up, 'cos I won't either.

"Love,

" Your gangster offspring,

"Amy Marie"

It was the most beautiful letter, and heartbreaking to re-read later. She had so much love in her heart, and was aware of the mistakes that she'd made. It seemed she really was determined to make a change in her life. We had high hopes for our middle child, and told many of our friends and family that things were improving with her.

Change was coming, but not exactly what Amy anticipated. She loved the house that we were living in and appreciated its easy access to downtown Okotoks and her friends, but we hadn't told her that we had actually signed a deal with a homebuilder to purchase his show home bungalow in 2009. The real estate market in Okotoks was red-hot at the time that we signed the deal (fall of 2007) and we were sure we could get a good price for our comfortable 5-bedroom, 2-storey house on the escarpment. The builder needed to show his home to the public for two years, then we could purchase it and move in for September of 2009.

We eventually told Amy about the purchase, with some trepidation, but she took the news quite well. Some things had changed in her life, and that may have influenced the way she reacted.

First of all, she had met Brandon. Brandon had been a "bad boy" during his teen years, even selling drugs at one time when his mom, Joanne, had separated from her husband and moved to a house in town with her boys. Mike even remembers buying pot from Brandon on one of the occasions that he and his musician friends decided to try smoking pot! However, Joanne had reconciled with her husband and moved back to the farm, and then Brandon decided to clean up and make something of himself.

He was the love of Amy's life. At the time, I believed that, if they could have stayed together, she probably would have given up drugs permanently and become a productive member of society. I know now that Amy had a lot more complicated problems than just drug use, and staying with any one man would not have fixed that. In fact, staying with just one man was impossible for her, because her issues always affected her relationships! I still fondly like to think sometimes, though, that Brandon was her soul mate and that she could have had a lifelong relationship with him.

The other thing that was going on in her life was that her job was not going well. She had somehow made a mistake at work and ended up costing Sam a lot of money, with the loss of a tattoo that he could have done for a customer. She never told me the details, but he did tell her that she had "cost him a tattoo". She was also partying more at this point, and was late for work on several occasions.

One Saturday, she went out drinking with some of her friends at night and didn't return home till the wee hours of the morning. She got up to go to work (late!) and returned home shortly after getting there, telling me that Sam had sent her home to sleep off her hangover, because she was no use to him at work. However, the next day, when she went in to work, he asked her,

"What are you doing here?"

Apparently, he had fired her on the Sunday and she hadn't got the message! She was now out of a job again, and so began the everyday search in the papers and weekly job interviews. At this point in her life, Amy said job interviews terrified her and she performed nervously, stuttering and answering questions wrongly.

Amy with her brother Michael, Christmas 2009

Amy Moves Back To The City

She never did find another job in Okotoks but, by the following spring, Brandon had found an apartment in Calgary and suggested that they move in together. I have to admit that I felt relief, as her constant unemployed presence in our house was starting to get on my nerves, and her inability to pay her share of the rent was seriously annoying me. She still continued to keep an untidy room and was no longer offering to help with dishes and cooking. She was reverting to her old behaviours from the last time she had lived with us, and my patience was running out. I kept up a good face, though, while somewhat looking forward to the day that she moved in to Calgary.

She moved in April. Brandon wasn't ready to move out of his parents' house, but he had a friend who would share the apartment with her until he could get there. His friend, John, was supposed to pay half of the rent and be company for her before Brandon could move in.

Amy had lined up some friends to help her move but, as so often happened with her friends, they all cancelled out at the last minute. So, one Monday night, she and I loaded up Ed's truck with her few bits of furniture and other paraphernalia and drove into Calgary. With John's help, we moved all of the furniture into the spacious, two-bedroom apartment on Macleod Trail, the only difficulty being the queen-size mattress, which wouldn't fit into the apartment elevator! The two of them were faced with carrying the mattress up 15 flights of stairs, until a kindly gentleman showed them how to stash it in the elevator so that it would fit. I breathed a sigh of relief when Amy advised me that it had been installed in the apartment!

Brandon moved in to the apartment one month later and John, whose girlfriend was now pregnant and wanting him to be with her, moved out. By this time, Amy couldn't stand John and they were not getting along at all, so she was relieved to have Brandon in the house! There began several months of "domestic bliss", or so Ed and I thought.

She even landed herself a job at another tattoo parlour, after being fired from the waitressing job she had first had when she moved into town. She had also tried two weeks at an esthetics school, as she had decided briefly to become a nail technician and learn to do women's gel and acrylic nails. However, she informed me that the school was "useless" and she wasn't learning anything, so Brandon convinced her to quit. This was her second attempt at post-high school education, and it was as successful as the first!

The second tattoo parlour was a great experience for her. She worked there for almost ten months and, during her employment there, she completed the full sleeve of tattoos that had been started by Sam on one arm, as well as a zodiac sign on her foot.

We attended a reception at the tattoo parlour one Sunday afternoon, at which Amy was the hostess and bartender. We met another couple there, whose son was one of the tattoo artists, and bonded with them over our children's artistic natures and love of the "fringe" lifestyle that goes with the tattoo world. The couple was also very interested in community theatre, and expressed an interest in attending one of our theatre productions in Okotoks. As I looked over at our beautiful daughter, I was proud of the way she was conducting herself and of how well-liked she seemed to be among the staff and artists in the shop. Brandon didn't attend, as he was home visiting his parents on the acreage, so we didn't connect with him that day.

However, at Christmas, which was held at my brother's house in north Calgary, he came with Amy and we had a wonderful family Christmas, with my mum, our Michael and Stephanie and her boyfriend, Mike. Stephanie and Mike were by now engaged. It was one of the happiest family Christmases we have ever had, and both of our daughters looked beautiful, while the young men were handsome and congenial. My mum and Brandon had a long conversation, which pleased me, as I was definitely at this point thinking of Brandon as possible son-in-law material (always the optimist!). Everyone got along well, and it was such a wonderful time. There is a photo of Amy with Ed, which was later shown in newspapers and on TV, with his arm around her, looking proud of his second daughter. In fact, that photo was cropped and used many times in the future, and remains our favourite photo of her to this day. She had spent Christmas Eve at Brandon's house and had a lovely time there, too. Joanne has since given me photos of that occasion, which I often look at fondly.

But all was not well in paradise. Come the following January, Amy and Brandon were having vicious arguments, which she said always ended in violence on his part towards her. (We never believed her based on what we knew of Brandon.) At one point, the police were called in by the anxious neighbours and, when they looked up Amy on their CPIC system, they discovered the outstanding warrants for shop-lifting, passing counterfeit and impersonation of her sister!

So Amy landed up in jail once again. Brandon phoned us and said she was being held on $1,000 bail, and Ed agreed to pay up. We sent Brandon the money and he got her out of jail, but the peace was short-lived. Although he found her a good defense lawyer (Mr. Charles Latimer, the one he had used when he was in trouble as a teenager), she would now have to go to court to reckon with her charges. Meanwhile, the two of them continued to have terrible fights.

That winter, Amy decided to sign up again for her great passion, the theatre. She auditioned for a series of one-act plays that our theatre group was putting on with the intention of entering a one-act festival. At the auditions, two directors were fighting over having her in their play: she was such a talented actress, and brought whole new levels to every part she played. She was finally cast in a two-person play with another actress, in which both girls had to play a total of nine parts (one of Amy's was a male character!) The play was directed by a friend of ours, Patrick, and both girls worked so hard. The play was a delight to watch.

However, on the day of the actual festival, Amy was nowhere in sight. I phoned her to see whether she was on her way to Okotoks to appear in her play, and she told me that she and Brandon were again fighting and he was refusing to drive her. I jumped in my car and went to pick her up from south Calgary, delivering her just in time to perform in the play. Patrick was very grateful, but later told us that working with her had been a nightmare. Her lack of dependability and reliability was only marginally outweighed by the brilliance she would show as soon as she stepped in front of the footlights.

As was the way with all of her relationships with men, the love affair was over and Brandon could no longer live with her. Her mercurial moods, her sudden outbursts of temper followed by protestations of love and threats of suicide when he said he would leave, drove him away and he finally left her at the end of the month.

She was devastated! She believed she really loved him and, although she usually ended her relationships hating the man she had once loved (at least, for a while), she always regretted breaking up with Brandon and tried several times to get back together with him. I guess she recognized the overall solidness and goodness of the man, and wanted that in her unstable, roller coaster life. We also regretted their breakup. I really liked Brandon and his mom, Joanne, and wished that we could somehow bring them back together. But by now we knew that there was something seriously wrong with Amy and it wasn't just hard drug use. She had been off the drugs for a while, but the fluctuating moods continued and she still seemed to be completely unreliable and unaware of her responsibilities.

She had been evicted from her apartment, due to the screaming, noisy fights with Brandon, and we helped her move into a duplex not far from there, which she shared with another man, a student at S.A.I.T.

She then lost her job at the tattoo parlour. She told me that it was because the owner was bringing one of his relatives in to do the receptionist's job, but she later admitted that, without Brandon there beside her to wake her up in the mornings, she was often late for work and her employers got tired of it. By February, she was unemployed and once again in the midst of the usually fruitless search for gainful employment. She was evicted from her apartment, due to noisy fights on the phone with Brandon and her roommate's inability to sleep through the arguments.

Amy "Amijane Marshall" in her dancing days

Amy Meets Greg

As summer approached, Amy met a man, Greg, who offered her a place to live. I'm not sure that he was a drug dealer, but he was certainly an addict, and obviously mentally ill. She didn't tell us much about him when she met him, only that he had offered her a room in his apartment and that she would be paying him rent as soon as she could find a job. I remember meeting her once in Calgary because she had asked us to pay her lawyer some money, as she could no longer pay his fees. Much against my better judgment, I gave her $500, but it was in the form of a cheque made out directly to the lawyer. I believe that she did actually forward it to Mr. Latimer, as it came back to me through the bank system, and didn't appear to have been tampered with. I really didn't like the idea of giving her a cheque of that size at the time, although I still naively believed that she wasn't back on drugs. It seemed too much like enabling.

After I handed her the cheque, I asked her to come with me to Stephanie's apartment, as Stephanie was having a "home party" for a cosmetic line and had invited both Amy and me. My younger daughter immediately became panicky, and started trying to get out of the car.

"Where are you going?" I demanded. "Why don't you want to come to Steph's with me?"

"My roommate won't let me go anywhere!" Amy replied in a scared voice. "If I don't come home exactly when I say I will, he locks me in a room and won't let me out!"

I was completely shocked and probably looked at her like she was from outer space. Hadn't she learned anything from Keith?

"Amy!" I asked her. "What are you doing living with this man, if he treats you like that?"

She immediately did an about-face.

"Well, it's not really all that bad," she replied. "He just gets mad if I'm late home."

"He shouldn't behave that way towards you," I told her. "If he makes a fuss about where you are and what time you come home, don't live with him!"

I thought I had brought my girls up to be independent with men, and not let them tell them what to do but, evidently in Amy's case, the message had not got through, as she seemed to have a habit of falling for and moving in with men who treated her disrespectfully, abusively in most cases. I tried to convince her to come with me to Stephanie's, but to no avail. She insisted that I drive her back to the LRT station, and said she would call me in a few days when I let her out of the car.

She didn't call me. In fact, the first time I spoke to her was after Brandon's mom called me and told me what was going on.

Apparently, things had got so bad with Greg, who was literally tying her up in the room that he allowed her to stay in, that things were reaching a crisis point. When he did let her out, he wanted to know exactly where she was, who she was talking to and when she would be home. He was keeping her a virtual prisoner in his home, and sounded like he was a nasty piece of work! A sick man, actually.

Well, Amy finally became frightened enough about his mental stability that she started texting and calling Brandon and begging him to come and rescue her. I don't know whether it was because she still loved him and it was a way to get back with him, or whether she felt that we wouldn't help her if she called us. Maybe she felt that we would simply be "too busy" (we did have very full lives of working full-time and being involved in theatre productions) to come and help her. Or perhaps she was just ashamed to admit the situation that she had got herself into.

At any rate, Brandon and his mom went to Greg's house and got Amy out of there while Greg was sleeping off a drug bender. They got her clothing and some of her possessions out, but the majority of her furniture and knick-knacks were left behind. They took her to stay on their acreage with them, and she called me the next day to tell me what had happened. It was like a covert operation, the way that they had effected her escape! I was very grateful to them but, at the same time, didn't feel that they should be obligated to keep her at their house, since she was no longer dating their son.

Brandon's mom, Joanne, really loved Amy and had always been very good to her. She was actually like a "second mother" to her. She seemed fine with the idea of Amy living with them, but I didn't think it was right. She was our responsibility, not theirs. When I spoke to Amy, who told me about her escape and how Greg had yelled at her and Joanne in a very threatening manner after they got her out and he realized what was going on, I suggested that she come back home and stay with us. She said she would, but she just wanted to stay with them for a few more days. She and Joanne were having good visits, and it seemed therapeutic for Amy to spend time with an older woman who was kind to her. Joanne also had a son who was struggling with drug addiction, so she had some knowledge of Amy's situation.

It was decided that Amy would come home to us on Father's Day and accompany us to Ed's parents' Father's Day barbecue. We all anticipated a lovely day, with our dear daughter safely returned to us and all of the family being so happy to have her come back into our midst. As usual, I was just fantasizing what I wanted to believe!

Amy Comes Home Once Again

Father's Day of 2010 dawned sunny and beautiful, and we all anticipated a pleasant day at my in-laws' house with all of the family.

Brandon brought Amy home in the late afternoon, just in time for us to drive to Calgary for dinner. We welcomed her home, and thanked him and his family for everything they had done for her. We also made arrangements to drive out to his parents' acreage and pick up the rest of her belongings during the week.

We got into the car around 4 o'clock to make the drive to Calgary, and Amy immediately demanded my cellphone. I refused (probably with the image in my mind of that terrible drive home at Christmas during the snowstorm!), and anyway, I figured that she could visit with her parents on the way in, rather than talking with her friends on the phone.

She immediately became incensed, and demanded my phone in louder and louder tones. We were barely down the road from our house when I reiterated "no" to her request for my phone. She then announced,

"Well, I'm not going with you, then!"

"What are you going to do?" I demanded. "We're not turning around and leaving you alone in the house while we're gone!" (We still didn't totally trust her not to steal money or belongings of ours, as past experience had made us wary.)

"I don't know, but I'm NOT going with you!" she yelled, jumping out of the car and heading back to our house.

Ed and I looked at each other. In the spirit of "tough love", we felt that we shouldn't go back and urge her to get into the car with the promise of giving her my phone, so we continued on to Calgary.

It was a fraught dinner with the family, spoiled by the scene with Amy. She called us several times during dinner, insisting on knowing when we would be back, but we told her that we would return when we were ready. Apparently, she had tried to break into the house through the basement, but the windows were a lot harder to force open than the ones at our old house (excellent new construction!). My neighbour, Brenda, later told me that she had knocked on their door and requested to use the washroom. Feeling guilty about the whole situation, I had apologized to my neighbour, but she said that Amy was "very sweet" and that there was nothing to apologize for.

We returned home to a very sullen Amy, who went straight to bed after we arrived. Nothing more was said about the unfortunate incident, other than my reminding her that, once I've said no to something, I'm not going to change my mind because someone has a tantrum. Famous last words, as I was to realize later!

Well, that night, the house phone started ringing. And it rang all night! Amy would answer it, scream her head off for a few minutes, then hang up or be hung up on. I ran down to the basement after the first couple of times and wanted to know who was calling in the middle of the night. She replied that it was Greg. I was completely puzzled. Hadn't she just been rescued from the abusive Greg, so why was she talking on the phone with him at all hours of the night?

This continued again the next night. The phone would be silent during the daytime and the evening, then would start ringing at about one in the morning. She would answer it immediately and the yelling would start. Sometimes she would come up to the kitchen and be screaming at Greg right outside our bedroom door. I soon learned to pick up the phone and tell Greg not to call in the middle of the night, but he would wait for half an hour and then it would all begin again.

We finally unplugged the phones in an attempt to prevent the calls, but then he would just call Amy on her cellphone! The situation was disrupting to our sleep and causing a lot of friction between Amy and us. I continually asked her why she would talk to a man who had abused her so badly, and she told me it was because she wanted her belongings back that were still at his apartment. I urged her to forget about them and that she could get new things, but Amy was never able to let go of her beloved possessions, and seemed to need to have them around her. Not being able to relinquish her belongings or the abusive men in her life was a pattern with her that I could never understand. I now know why she behaved like that, but the whole thing was extremely puzzling then.

I had called Greg once on my cellphone to tell him to stop calling Amy, and then he started texting me, telling me that he was basically a good man and he did have a heart. He promised to be at home, if we were to make the trip downtown, and we could pick up her remaining furniture and clothing.

Well, we made the trip, but of course, he wasn't home when he said he would be! I think Amy and I made a total of three trips and never did get her things back. After several loud phone calls with him, she made him angry and he deliberately left her furniture (which he had thrown on the lawn in a fit of temper, exactly as Mark had done) out in the rain. After that, the phone calls and texts slowed down and eventually stopped. I later learned that she did, in fact, press charges against him for imprisoning and abusing her physically and she did go to court for it, but I never learned the outcome.

Amy was still dealing with the court system and lawyers because of her shop-lifting and impersonation charges, so we had made it our mission to get her to court for her trial. She had only been home a week when we had to take her in to Calgary for a 9 a. m. court date. Now Amy was a night owl, and had always had trouble getting up in the morning, so I started waking her up at around 6:45 a.m., with the plan to leave at 8. After the third wake-up call, she started getting angry with me and, by 7:30, was actively yelling at me and calling me names. I didn't give up, as I knew that being late for court often means a contempt of court charge, so I was becoming more and more anxious.

She finally got out of bed, but took her time getting ready, and I went down to the basement several times in an effort to chivy her up. She became increasingly incensed with me and finally came up the stairs, but still wasn't ready. When I finally shouted at her that we needed to leave "right this minute!" she angrily threw her high-heeled shoe on the hardwood floor on the main floor, leaving a huge dent in the wood. To this day, we can see the hole left by her shoe, and it is a sad reminder of the turmoil that we suffered when she came to live with us that last time.

We finally got to court, only to have the date put off by another three months, and this was to go on for at least a year. Putting court dates off by three months on several occasions is nothing unusual in our court system. Sometimes, it's to await the appearance of a key witness with evidence, sometimes it's because the judge needs more time to read some important background material, but often we weren't given a reason. We were becoming increasingly disenchanted with the legal system, and felt that much of our time had been wasted (time at work for which we would have been paid but, since we wanted to support our daughter, we willingly sacrificed). Also, what about the costs of continually summoning the same lawyers and clerks when there are so many cases waiting to be heard? Why not just get the case settled the first time?

Mr. Latimer had very kindly agreed to continue defending her, although she hadn't paid him anything since the time I had given her the cheque for his services. I did advance him two more cheques during the course of the litigation, but he was never fully paid for his services. It is a credit to him that he was very generous towards us, and he later told us that he always liked Amy and wanted to see her "smarten up". He once admitted to almost having wanted to take her home to live with him and teach her how to be a decent member of society. At the time, I thought it was very sweet of him, but I know now that merely living with someone who would try to keep her in line wouldn't cure Amy's antisocial behaviour.

Stephanie continued to be very angry with us because of our continued harbouring of Amy at our house. Carla even gave me a book on "enabling" and it was clear that she sided with her god-daughter in disapproving of our leniency. My own mother told me that I should be letting Amy go out on her own again and suffer the consequences of her behaviour, rather than allowing her to her continue to mark time in our home.

Indeed, she certainly didn't try to get a job, and in fact used to spend four-day weekends in Calgary with a friend of hers, Joe, and his girlfriend. I began to suspect that she was using crystal meth when she was with them, as she would come home and usually sleep for two days, then be very irritable and grouchy when she finally woke up. I had no proof of the drug use, and she of course denied it, but the thought kept niggling away at the back of my mind.

That summer, we were going on holiday with my mum, who often came out to visit in the summer, to a friend's condo in beautiful Osoyoos, B.C.. Amy apparently had a friend, Mark, in Kelowna, who invited her out to visit him for a week and she was very anxious to go. After her dismissal from the tattoo parlour, we had been able to get unemployment benefits for her and she had just received a cheque from the government. True to form, she immediately wanted to spend all of the money on a holiday. I had yet another argument with her, trying to convince her to pay rent and put the rest of the money away in a savings account but, like a spoiled child who wants what she wants, she threw a huge temper tantrum until we allowed her to keep the money. With my poor mum there, I just didn't want to have any more screaming arguments in the house, so I gave in. So much for my insistence that, once I had said no,

I wouldn't change my mind! More enabling.

The plan was for Amy to drive with us to Kelowna, and we even arranged hotel rooms there for Mum and ourselves so that we could stay over after we dropped her off. Well, Amy ended up going to Joe's and not being able to get back to Okotoks in time for us to leave on the Saturday morning we were due to leave. When I phoned her, she calmly told us that she would just take a bus to Kelowna and that Mark would meet her at the other end.

Well, in true Amy form, she booked the bus for the wrong day and ended up not being able to go to Kelowna for two more days. There was always chaos any time she tried to organize anything, and this occasion was no exception. Mark was quite distressed about her failure to arrive on time, and they had several tumultuous phone calls. However, Mark – like so many of the men in Amy's life – was in love with her, and was willing to forgive her anything once she turned up.

I believe that she loved him, too, and always would. However, at the time, she was still healing from Brandon and wasn't ready for a relationship with Mark. She enjoyed her week with him and his family, and the photos from the holiday show a very happy girl. She even started posting her status on Facebook as "married", but I don't think she really meant anything by that at the time. The wonderful thing about Mark was that he just loved her, without demanding anything from her, and always allowed her to be the way she was. That was to come to mean a lot to her later on but, at this stage, she wasn't ready to include him fully in her life.

We had a horribly long drive to Osoyoos, complicated by the fact that we had to go to Kelowna first, instead of taking the shorter route there, and I was very upset by the time we arrived there late at night. Once again, Amy had put us out with her thoughtless behaviour and I was starting to really lose patience with her.

We picked her up on the way back from our holiday, and she drove us crazy most of the way back by continually opening the rear truck window while we were on the highway, which then caused the window to vibrate noisily. Repeated requests to her to close the window were then ignored - it was like the Christmas snowstorm all over again! Finally, I told her to change places with me and sit in the front of the truck. After that, she calmed down and was mostly pleasant for the rest of the trip.

In the lake with Mark, Kelowna, BC, summer 2010

We Show Amy The Door Again

That summer, Amy had participated in a sort of beauty pageant in Calgary, which was put on by the cover rock band *Suicide Blonde,* which was looking for a "mascot" to represent them. The pageant took place over two days and was held in Calgary.

She asked us to support her in her efforts, and we agreed. We knew that she and several other girls would be strutting around in skimpy outfits, but it was important to her and she had been assured by the band's manager that she would be a "shoo-in' to win the contest, if she entered.

Stephanie wasn't at all happy about our supporting Amy in this, as she said that Amy participating in a beauty pageant would simply glorify women with skinny bodies, and that this would contribute to her eating disorder. She would then continue to use drugs in order to stay skinny. Having an eating disorder was only one facet of her mental health problems, although she did in fact say that it was the only thing wrong with her during another attempt by us to get her into a rehab facility in Calgary. She told the counselor that she didn't have a drug problem, but an eating disorder, and thus sabotaged being admitted to that particular rehab. She was given forms to attend the Eating Disorder Clinic at the Children's Hospital, and at the time I couldn't understand how this would stop her crystal meth use. She never followed up with the Children's Hospital, and I once again lost patience with her and basically gave up on trying to get her into rehab. She would only lie to the counselors about what was wrong with her, so why bother?

But I digress. We did attend the beauty pageant on the first night, and Amy was advanced to the second round. There were a lot more of her friends and supporters on the second night, and one of them was Brandon's mom, Joanne. We were very pleased to see her, and she and I really bonded over our love for our beautiful and talented, though troubled, daughter. Joanne remains a friend, and has kept in touch on some special occasions involving Amy since then.

Well, Amy won the pageant, and not just on her beauty and ability to dance, but because she embodied the band's requirement for a mascot, with her sassy and engaging attitude. She was awarded a cowboy hat, an electric guitar, a round-trip to Las Vegas (which she couldn't unfortunately avail herself of due to the criminal charges against her), $500 worth of coupons to restaurants and bars associated with the venue where the pageant was held, and $500 to be given to charity. She chose the Calgary Women's Shelter, as one who had often suffered abuse at men's hands. She was always very empathic towards women who suffered from domestic abuse, although she continued to court it in many of her own relationships.

Life became very difficult that fall, with Amy going every Thursday through Monday to Joe's house and returning during the week to sleep it off. She gave up the search for employment, and her room started to look more like a tornado went through it with each passing day. Repeated requests to tidy it up and to go for some job interviews were at first ignored, and then the temper would erupt after the requests were repeated.

She still continued to receive unemployment cheques from the government, but we saw no rent payments from them. I was starting to suspect in earnest that all of her money was going on drug use and partying with Joe and his friends. My frustration levels were rising, and I was starting to resent her presence in our house, much as I had done the last time she came home and was living there fruitlessly every day. Only that time, she moved into the city with Brandon – now she had nowhere to go!

Halloween approached, and we had been invited to a party at our friend Fiorentina's house. Amy announced that there would be a party for the rock band who had held the beauty pageant on Halloween, and that she would be attending in the role of their mascot. It was to be her first appearance representing them and she should have been excited about it.

However, as the time came closer, she did nothing to prepare for the upcoming event and I became more and more agitated as I thought about it. I had also received more phone calls from Stephanie, Carla and my mum urging me to not let her stay with us any more, since we were probably enabling her in her drug use. Amy always denied it when I questioned her, and I continued to support her to my family members. This was causing estrangement between Stephanie and me.

Well, the day of Halloween, Amy slept until about three in the afternoon and, when I questioned her about the party the band was putting on, she said, "Oh, I'm not going to that. I think I'm just going to stay here for the weekend and rest."

Well, maybe she was trying to avoid going to Joe's place again and using crystal meth, I will never know, but I saw red. Several months of frustration with her and her inability to get on with her life, coupled with the obligation I knew that she had towards the band, made me get really angry. I think I had reached the breaking point and could no longer tolerate her in our house. (Also, we didn't want to miss Fiorentina's party!) Having Amy alone in the house, getting up to who knows what, was not a good option.

"You are going to Calgary!" I told her in a cold tone. "You have an obligation to the band, and you can't let them down."

"I don't care!" She replied defensively. "I'm not going. I just want to stay here and rest."

"Well, I don't want you here!" I snapped, my temper escalating. "You get your things packed and go to Calgary. They're expecting you at the Halloween party!"

"I'm not going!" she screeched. "And you can't make me!"

"Get going!" I snarled. "Get your things organized and I want you on your way to Calgary before we leave for the party tonight!"

Her reply was to pick up one of her heavy, high-heeled stilettos off the floor and throw it at my head, calling me horrible names while she did it. It hit me, although it didn't really hurt. I yelled at her again to get ready to leave, and she started picking up random items off the floor and throwing them at me. I fled, shutting the bedroom door after me, and she responded by locking the door.

Shaking all over, I went upstairs and told Ed what had happened.

"I don't care how she does it, but she has to go to Calgary!" I blubbered. "She has to go! She has an obligation to the band, and anyway I don't want her here. She's violent, and things will only get worse!"

Ed agreed with me, and I finally convinced him that, since he was stronger than Amy and would be a match for her if she started resisting or throwing things, he should get her into his truck and drive her to Calgary. He agreed, though reluctantly, and I left for our friend's party while he got our daughter sorted out.

He arrived at the party around eight o'clock and informed me that he had driven her to Calgary, as requested. I breathed a sigh of relief, but couldn't really enjoy the party for the rest of the night, as I was torn between relief at her being made to fulfill her obligation and guilt at the harsh words I had leveled at her.

However, by the next day, my resolve had deepened. Convinced that she was back on crystal meth and strengthened by my family's entreaties to stop enabling her, I suggested to Ed that we pack all of Amy's things and take them to storage. He agreed. I think he had come to the end of his road with her, too. Life had been a chaotic rollercoaster since she came back to live with us, and it was causing too much tension in the house. Besides, a girl her age should be making her own living, not living with her parents. Also, if she really did still have a drug problem, then she should get it treated.

So we packed up all of her belongings and moved them to storage. I was then able to finally clean the room that had been neglected for four months. It was disgusting! Dirt, hair and dust balls were underneath the clothes and furniture, mould had grown in the food under the bed and behind the night table, and there were makeup stains on the carpet and walls. I cleaned for two days to return the room to its original shape, although it was never quite the same again! Those stains on the carpet have never come out.

Meanwhile, Ed called Amy and told her that we had moved all of her things out, due to the violent behaviour that she had once again displayed towards her mother. Her response was shock, and then the usual expletives began. Exasperated, he hung up on her.

I noticed on Facebook that one of the band members had chastised her for not showing up to their Halloween gig. Even after Ed had taken her into Calgary, she had ditched the party and let them down! She probably just went to Joe's and indulged in her favourite habit. We felt justified in our actions.

Rock band "Suicide Blonde" featuring Amy

Transitions

After Amy went back to Calgary, we received a phone call from her telling us that we would never see her again and we would no longer be a part of her life. She also "unfriended" me on Facebook. It wasn't really surprising, but it still hurt, and I hoped that my daughter would eventually forgive us and include us in her life again, as she had before after countless fights. We still felt that we had done the right thing in moving her out, though, and hoped against hope that she would seek help for her addiction.

It was only a week later that she called me and told me she missed us. She said that she was living temporarily with Darren, a friend of Joe's, in southeast Calgary, and she wanted me to come and see the apartment, bringing some of her belongings with me. I agreed, and we had a pleasant visit that day. I asked her to re-friend me on Facebook (it was a good way of keeping up with what she was doing from day to day), and she agreed. We also hugged and made up the fight, although she told me that I had hurt her when I said that I didn't want her in our house. I apologized, but justified myself by saying that I was only trying to get her to go to the gig with the rock band. Although that was partially true, I didn't want to let on to her that I had become completely fed up with her behaviour and really did want her out of the house. Just how much does a parent of an adult child owe that child, when it comes to protection and shelter? It's a question about which I'm still struggling.

Well, things didn't work out with Darren. He very quickly got fed up with Amy "mooching" off him, not working and eating all of his food. He kicked her out, and she was once again homeless.

However, that didn't last long. She had been trying to find work and had eventually been hired by a dance group in Calgary. They were "gogo" dancers and, although they did wear skimpy outfits, they were not strippers, but exotic dancers, and they hired Amy because of her looks and her ability to dance. We were not completely happy with her situation, as there was always an element of suspicion in the back of our minds that they were in fact strippers, but we could never prove that. Stephanie certainly felt that it was true! (We have since been told by some of Amy's friends that she was too prudish to be a stripper. My stern teaching on the importance of modesty had evidently paid off! Also, having since met some of the dancers and their manager, we now know that they are definitely not strippers.)

The dancers offered Amy a place to stay, and she had temporary shelter for a while, moving from one girl's apartment to another, depending on how long it took for the hostess to become fed up with her refusal to comply with house rules.

Eventually, she announced that she had met a new man, Rick, at one of the dance clubs. She seemed very taken with him, and he was trying to get her involved in fitness, which was one of his passions. As she was dancing for a living, that seemed very appropriate, and we were impressed that this young man was making a project out of keeping Amy in good physical shape.

One morning, I opened up Facebook, and was surprised to find a long message from a man whom I didn't know.

It started, "Good morning, and pleased to meet you. You don't know me, but I'm a friend of Amy's and I need your help."

The writer of the message was Rick. He was struggling with daily life with Amy, and couldn't understand why she would almost purposely start a fight with him, then escalate it to levels of hysteria where she was sobbing and screaming insults at him, blaming him for all the troubles that had ever befallen her in her life, only to then protest undying love and begging his forgiveness if he threatened to break up with her.

I thought about what he wrote, and ruminated on it that day before I replied to his message. We had seen this behaviour before with her and suddenly I was sure that I had figured out why it was happening again. Now that she was back in the city, Amy once again had easy access to crystal meth, and obviously she had fallen back into her old ways of drug use (if she had ever stopped!). She was probably purchasing it with the wages she made from dancing.

I told Rick that Amy had a problem, and that he could help her (and his relationship with her) by taking her to rehab. I explained that we had tried on several occasions, but had never been really successful. I thought that maybe he stood a better chance of getting her there, because of her affection for him.

She called us a few days later and told us that she was going to the Renfrew detox centre, and that Rick would take her there. She had then applied to go to "Servants Anonymous", a rehab facility which was aimed towards women who had been involved with the sex trade and, since she was doing exotic dancing for a living, she would qualify to go there.

We were very happy to hear that she had finally decided to meet her problem head on and to do something about it, and that Rick was supportive of her efforts. We thought that she had a chance to make something of her life, as the programme she was entering was six months long, and they would even help her to find work after she finished there. She did her ten days at detox, then entered the facility at Servants Anonymous to begin her rehabilitation.

She was allowed out at weekends and stayed with Rick. She would often come to dinner at our house on Sundays, bringing him with her, and we all liked him. Stephanie would pick them up and we would often drive them back, and he always seemed like a nice, friendly guy, who worked for a living and paid his rent. He was responsible, and seemed to genuinely care for Amy, so we were happy that he was in her life. He always made sure that she returned to Servants Anonymous in time for her curfew of 11 p.m.

She called us often from there, and Rick also kept us posted on her progress. At first, it seemed to be going very well, and she loved all of the women who worked at the facility, although she sometimes felt that the other girls living there didn't like her. She didn't get involved in any out-and-out fights, but some of the girls made her feel uncomfortable about herself.

It wasn't very long before she hated the place! She said that they made her eat all of the meals that they prepared, and that she was gaining weight. She also wasn't allowed to wear her beloved hair extensions, and it was an ongoing argument every day when she came down to breakfast wearing them. The ladies tolerated it for a while, but then repeatedly warned her that she would have to leave if she persisted in breaking the rules.

She became more and more sullen as time wore on, and said that she just wanted out of rehab. We urged her to stick with the programme, and so did Rick.

Here is an excerpt from a diary that we found later among her things, in which she addresses her life there and her self-image. She also hints at the eating disorder that she had told me she had the last time she went to rehab:

107

"May 9, 2011

"I have decided to name this journal "The Endangered Thoughts of One Miss Ami Jane, Part II" as a second attempt of actual thought journaling. It is not only my second attempt, but the second time where I shall attempt logging on paper without fear of this book being stolen and used against me. I name it after the first and hope, per se, this much like the first edition will help you just like it did me.

"Although the title now missiles my brain through several unwanted past memories, and I am once again reminded of the only picture I had of one past love (Keith) and can recall it in sick descriptive detail and am fondly reminded of the intoxicated Cheshire grins on both of our faces. I am also brought to memory of those times.

"I will now try to bring myself back to the now. As it is almost five years since, and I am needing to live in the present and no longer dwell on past ridiculousness. I am 26. I still act like I am 16 and am almost less responsible than I was at that age. Mind you, I have been heartbroken, beaten and sold back more times than both ages put together (I kid!), but in all reality I feel near 40.

"I am yet again in recovery. Almost 60 days clean and 40 lbs. heavier. I need to get past this obsession!

"I am, this go-round of sobriety, in treatment, kicking and screaming, as usual packing my bags twice a day, threatening to leave, only to make the days shorter. My theory is insane, much like the rest of my life, but isn't that what N. A. tells us?

"At this time, I am more devoted to working my programme seriously, now more than ever. I do still contemplate faking sobriety again, but look where that got me. On that note, perhaps I will go into minor detail as to why. They always say it gets harder, deeper, faster, each relapse. This time, you can bet your last nickel it was! I can now add junkie to my list of "dids" and I must have put that one out to the universe much like I did battered "wife", criminal and vagrant. I now find myself in an amazing programme. It deals with girls who were involved or at risk of the sex trade – lucky me, I qualified! Upon entering, I still believed love from someone else might save me, now I am coming to understand that the only love that can save me must come from within. I must dig deep down, pull out the ice chipper even, and try to find the heart within me and learn how to love myself. My whole self, not just "Suicide Barbie" that lives within me.

"She, sadly, is my not so better half. The one I chose to feed more most days, therefore she is much stronger a personality than me. Amy Sands – not even Amijane Marshall, my alter ego. I'm not letting on that I have multiple personalities, but

referencing a great story I read today about wolves – one evil one, one good – the battle that one creates inside one's head. She who will win is the one you feed more.

"I have lived daily for at least a year creating myself into a person I no longer recognize. I am afraid to be myself because I really forgot who I am, living behind a spray tanned, lash-glued, hair-extensioned glamour queen who only eats four times a week. I exaggerate, but I am more open about these masks because I am able to see the real difference now. I was lost and I'm still lost, but I feel much better now, seeing the girl who I really am. I often try to pretend she doesn't exist, mostly out of fear and rejection. I found people liked me more when "Suicide Barbie" is in control. I've also begun to accept this too is false. The N.A. saying "Tell Yourself" now always comes to mind when I begin to think like that again.

(Note: this is a reference to the rock band whose name contained the word suicide)

May 10, 2011

"The time is quarter to nine. I find myself sitting in class at Phase 2 today. I slept not as great as I would have liked, and my 6:30 wake-up call came much too early.

May 16, 2011

"Today is a day to remember – it is my 60 days clean! Time goes by so slowly clean. I consider relapse more and more daily. I have gained about 40 lbs., *which I am not okay with. I grow more and more resentful of the programme I am in now, knowing that I never would have put it on in the first place. I knew rehab was a stupid idea! I've put everything in place, shall I choose to relapse only for 10 lbs.' sake. Maybe it is better, it may not be as tedious as before.*

May 26, 2011

"The weather has been dreary for days now, the rain is bringing the world into summer quicker than imagined. It has also brought spring fever my direction and cold season is upon us. This is the first cold I've been hit with in two years – I forgot what it felt like to be ill! The joy of sobriety! On the contrary, the days are going by much easier as of late. It has been almost three months' strong in this programme. I made a solemn vow to swallow my pride and bite my tongue and make my own life easier, by obeying the rules and requests here. I feel like a stranger in my own figure because of it, but I know that it will be something worthy of my attempt. I grew to not know the girl under all the glam and forgot what it was like to once again be the girl I had grown up as. My face reminds me of an older version of the girl back in high school. It is very strange to me. I feel as though my style and uniqueness is

gone by the wayside, but this is only because of having to make do with what I have. Most of my recent wardrobe is simply out of "guess these pants will do if they fit" and try to ensemble mix and matched randoms.

"The tanner has been becoming minimal on a daily basis, and I'm finding my hair extensions don't suit me any more … but neither does this yellow bob that refuses to hold any style. I've been contemplating returning to being a brunette as of late because I just don't enjoy the blond anymore. I don't feel sassy. This leads my mind to wander, of course. It wants my reaction to running back to the old ways again, but nothing will ever change for me if I never change my ways. I have grown to instant-gratify my insecurities. Sobriety takes time. This isn't a race, I must remind myself . . . there is more to life than being a supermodel.

"There is more to me than just skin deep perfection. The run-in with the dreaded detox love the other day at Tim's was nearly fatal to me. I felt so awkward and swollen. He almost looked down at me, it seemed. I was so nervous that I'm sure I appeared to be spun, but it was only nerves that had me riled up . . . "
(She had bumped into someone with whom she'd had a brief relationship at a previous detox stay.)

And it ends there, never completed.

Poor Amy! She just couldn't stick with the programme at Servants Anonymous. Just shortly after she wrote this, she broke curfew one weekend and was asked to leave. She called Rick and he picked her up, taking her back to live with him at his apartment (much against his better judgment, as he was really angry with her for sabotaging her rehab), as she had nowhere else to go.

Amy Moves On

Rick couldn't put up with her for more than two weeks, as expected. At the end of that time, they had a huge fight and he threw her things out on the lawn, locking her out of the house – much as Mark had done! He felt terrible about it, and called us to explain, but he just couldn't live with her moods.

She told me that she had only gone to rehab to please him, not for herself and, until you decide to manage your addiction for yourself, you are never going to be able to beat it. Although she didn't admit to being back on drugs, we suspected that that was what was happening.

She also said that she thought Rick was cheating on her, with his next-door neighbour. She asked us to let her come back home again, but we refused. She hung up on me when I said no, and I felt terrible at the time, but I was committed to no longer enabling her.

She always seemed to land on her feet. Before long, she had found shelter with another friend, a lady named Julia. Julia lived downtown, in a nice apartment, and she seemed very kind to Amy. She was an attractive older woman, who dressed in style and was very friendly. She was divorced, and apparently had four children, although they hadn't lived with her for many years.

She took Amy in, and the two of them seemed to get along well at first. I was happy that Amy seemed to have found another "second mother", like Joanne, and I thought that she was now set up. She even tried to find work, as she was living in the heart of the business area on 17th Avenue, and I thought I could breathe again when it came to worrying about her. Little did I know that Julia was not what she seemed, and I still had reason to worry about our daughter.

She decided to start dancing again, to make some rent money, but that wasn't going very well for her. She said that the other girls judged her appearance and that she was too heavy for dancing (she was in the process of shedding the 40 lbs. that she had gained in rehab). She then made the decision to attend Delmar College, with the intention of becoming a hairdresser, like her sister. I expressed surprise that she didn't want to pursue her massage studies again, but she assured me that hairdressing would suit her better.

She applied to the college and was accepted, and Ed set about releasing the money from the RESP that we had saved for her since she was a baby. It wouldn't be enough money for her fees, but the understanding was that she would get student loans to cover the balance. He had several conversations with the college, and it all seemed to be going well.

She and Julia moved to another location, we weren't sure why, but they continued with their arrangement while Amy went to Delmar. She complained on occasion that Julia had loud parties and wanted Amy to participate in them, when she was supposed to be studying, and then she would finally abandon her studies and join the party.

My mum was out visiting us again that summer and, one day, we were going to Calgary to do some shopping. I gave Amy a call and asked whether we could visit her, as Mum would like to see her while she was in town. Amy agreed but, as we were getting nearer to downtown, she suddenly called and asked us if we could meet her at a nearby café, as Julia wanted her out of the house.

We agreed, and met Amy shortly thereafter. My mum was shocked at her appearance! She had lost all the weight she gained in rehab by now, and was looking very scrawny again. Her hair was once again brunette, but very messy and untidy for someone who was in hairdressing school. Her makeup was smudged, her mood was bad, and our conversation with her was difficult.

She told Mum and me that school was not going well, as many of the girls disliked her, and she wasn't sure she was going to stick with it. It seemed like high school and massage college all over again.

We drove her back to Julia's apartment building after our coffee, and Mum expressed concern over her.

"Do you think she's on drugs again?" she asked me.

"I honestly couldn't tell you, Mum," I replied. "She tells me she's going to school, and that Julia is a good roommate, but I don't know what to think, seeing her like that."

We were both left with a very uneasy feeling about what was happening with Amy.

Not long after that, I again went to see her at the apartment and met Julia walking into the building with a man.

"Was that Julia's boyfriend?" I asked Amy afterwards, when she walked me to my car.

"Yes," she replied quickly, looking away from me as she answered. I had a feeling that she was not telling me something, but I just couldn't put my finger on it at the time.

It was many months later that Amy finally told me that Julia was an escort, and that she had tried to get Amy to join her in "the lifestyle". The time that she had asked Amy to meet Mum and me at a café was because she was entertaining a client in the apartment. Apparently, Amy didn't succumb to joining Julia in her lifestyle choice, but she did admit to having had a "sugar daddy" at one time.

Not long after, as had happened before, Amy dropped out of Delmar College, after they informed her that she hadn't been to class regularly enough to be able to continue with the course. The Director called us and told us that she seemed very "distracted" in her life, but that they would welcome her back in the fall, if she managed to get her life back on track. He was being very kind, as I'm sure he suspected what was really going on, but he did give her the benefit of the doubt.

She told us that she was going to go back to dancing again, and for a while things went along fairly smoothly. However, as always happened with Amy, that was going to be short-lived.

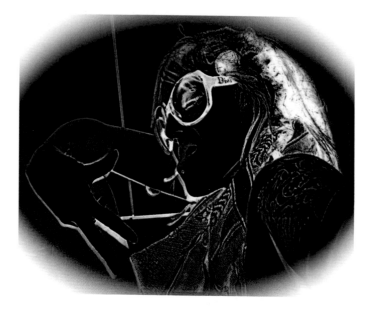

Amijane dance interpretation

Amy Meets "Bad Rick"

A few months later, Amy called to tell us that she had a new boyfriend, whom she had apparently met through Julia (we were still blissfully unaware of Julia's lifestyle, and believed that she was helping our daughter by letting her live with her. It should be mentioned, however, that Julia loved Amy a lot and often tried to help her with the situations that she got herself into). Amy announced plans to move to a new apartment, as she felt that things weren't really working out with Julia. Anyway, she was in love with this new man, whose name was also Rick , and she wanted to spend time with him without Julia being in the background. Julia was also moving again, and would be living in the next building.

So Amy moved to a nice little walk-up apartment in Mount Royal and, on one of my trips to Calgary, I went to visit her and there met the new Rick. He seemed quiet, and quite a nice person. He shook my hand warmly, and was very polite to me, so I was quite willing to approve of this new boyfriend and hope for the best. She told me at the time that he worked for the City of Calgary as a pipefitter, and I believed her.

She was very much in love once again, and I wanted her to be happy. However, not long after that, she called to say that they had had a terrible fight and he had been verbally abusive to her. I expressed concern, and told her that she shouldn't stay with a man who was abusive, and she agreed with me. They broke up, but it wasn't very long before they were back together again.

The pattern of having huge fights and breaking up, then getting back together again seemed to continue throughout their entire relationship, just as it did with the other men in her life. The abuse was also becoming physical, and she often called to tell us that he had beaten her. We urged her to get him out of her life, and to go to a shelter for abused women, if necessary. At one time, she confessed to me that Rick was a member of a gang, and she seemed proud of the fact. My mouth dropped open, but something in me didn't completely believe her. I think I just thought that she was trying to shock me, as Rick had seemed nice when I met him, and certainly didn't look like a gang member (whatever they are supposed to look like!).

Around this time, I happened to be at my doctor's office for a visit. Dr. Andrews had seen Amy on a couple of different occasions to fill out rehab forms for her, and I told him about the last failed attempt and our past unsuccessful efforts to bring her back home.

"I don't know what's wrong with her," I said, in frustration. "She has never been able to stick with rehab, she's impossible to get along with and seems to prefer to hang out with criminals! She certainly wasn't raised that way!"

"I think she has Borderline Personality Disorder," he told me. I looked at him in confusion. What was this disorder I'd never heard of, and how come it had taken until Amy turned 26 before anyone recognized it? She had been in the psychiatric ward and to rehab on several occasions, but nobody had ever said anything about this!

"Look it up on the Internet when you get home," he replied. "I think you'll find that the description fits her. It will go a long way to explaining her behaviour."

So I went home and did just that. The first thing I saw was: "Are you living with chaos? Does your partner make you think you're crazy?"

Of course, this was supposed to apply to a spouse or partner, but it was sounding so familiar that I continued reading. I remembered Amy telling me that I was crazy when she was just a teenager, and our therapist assuring me that it was only what I was living with that was crazy, not me personally. The article outlined the signs and symptoms of Borderline Personality Disorder (BPD), and it fit Amy to a "t". The pieces had all fallen into place! It explained everything – her sudden mood swings, the chaotic lifestyle, the frantic outbursts of temper, the courting of the criminal side of life, the sworn hatred followed by a quick return to loving someone, the binge eating and substance abuse, even to the sudden change as a baby from being happy and content to screaming her head off within seconds. I even wondered whether the unusual labour that I had gone through with her had anything to do with it! There was no question in our minds that Amy had the disorder and, when we mentioned it to Stephanie, who was studying psychology in university at the time,she replied that, when she was studying borderline personality disorder, Amy's picture "could have been up on the wall". We had been suspecting that Amy had a mental illness for a few years now, as nothing seemed to explain her erratic moods and often outrageous behaviour.

I had mentioned earlier that Michael thought she was bipolar, but I hadn't really agreed with him that that was the problem. I had believed that everything up to this point was due to drug use, but I should have gone back further and reexamined her frequently odd behaviour, even during childhood. It was classic for this disorder, and I have to credit Dr. Andrews for figuring it out.

My mum (a former physician) didn't really agree with me when I told her about it on the phone, but mostly because she had never heard of the disorder. She then looked it up on the Internet, and phoned to tell me that, in her opinion, Amy fulfilled all of the nine criteria of BPD. She definitely concurred with her colleague on the diagnosis.

However, the down side of all of this was that I had also read that there was no real treatment for the disorder. There were some drugs available that could help with the mood swings, but really nothing that would "cure" the problem. Although knowing what was wrong with Amy did go a long way to helping us understand her, it meant that there was no real way to deal with her issues.

When we told Amy about it, she was at first upset, but then soon admitted that she did feel exactly as sufferers of BPD do (the intense fear of abandonment, the chronic feelings of emptiness and low self-worth, the unstable relationships). However, she was not ready to seek treatment, and indeed it was something that she avoided for the rest of her life – as a lot of BPD sufferers will do.

We had already learned the hard way that people with mental health issues will not receive successful treatment unless they realize that they need it and are committed to seeking help. Although Amy finally believed us that she had BPD, she wasn't willing to look for a treatment facility that could help her. At the time, we didn't know of any clinics that could successfully deal with the disorder anyway, so it was a matter of being relieved to have a diagnosis, but not knowing what to do about it.

Note: Amy seemed to have a pattern in her life - two Ricks and two Marks.

Amy at the lake in Kelowna, BC

Borderline Personality Disorder

From the reading that I've done on the disorder in the last couple of years since Amy's death, I'm convinced that Dr. Andrews was right in his diagnosis. According to the DSM 1V (American Diagnostic and Statistical Manual of Mental Disorders, Fourth Edition), there are nine behavioural indicators which usually define Borderline Personality Disorder. The name "Borderline" is a bit misleading, I think, and it could explain why Amy felt upset when we first told her about it.

"What? I'm a borderline person?!" She questioned me, hurt and dismay on her face.

I hastened to explain that it didn't have anything to do with her as a person. In fact, the reason Ed was given by one of his patients, who is a psychologist, for the name is that the symptoms straddle both neurosis and psychosis. A neurosis is a mild mental disorder, often involving anxiety, which sometimes incapacitates the sufferer (e.g, a phobia, or obsessive-compulsive behaviour). A psychosis, on the other hand, is a serious mental disorder that causes the sufferer to lose touch with reality. The description "borderline" reflects the opinion of most clinicians that their patients' behaviours are on the border between these two mental conditions.

The nine behavioural indicators, according to DSM-IV-TR, are as follows:

1. Frantic efforts to avoid real or imagined abandonment

2. Unstable and intense interpersonal relationships

3. Lack of clear sense of identity

4. Impulsiveness in potential self-damaging behaviours, such as substance abuse, sex, shoplifting, reckless driving, binge eating

5. Recurrent suicidal threats or gestures, or self-mutilating behaviours

6. Severe mood shifts and extreme reactivity to situational stresses

7. Chronic feelings of emptiness

8. Frequent and inappropriate displays of anger

9. Transient, stress-related feelings of unreality or paranoia

These symptoms are grouped into four primary areas for which treatment can be sought:

1. Mood instability

2. Impulsivity and dangerous uncontrolled behaviour

3. Interpersonal psychopathology

4. Distortions of thought and perception

Amy had certainly exhibited the mood instability right from a young child, and this only became worse when the teenage years hit. In fact, one article I read said that sufferers of BPD usually "brutalize" their families! She had also indulged in impulsive and dangerous behaviours, including her crime-filled life with Keith, and her use of drugs and alcohol. She had indulged in substance abuse, promiscuous sex, shoplifting, reckless driving and binge eating (this is why I think she didn't really have an eating disorder as such, but rather that this was a symptom of her BPD. She lacked the frequent perfectionism of eating disorder sufferers. However, an argument could be made that the frequent bullying about her weight when she was a young child could have promoted an eating disorder). She had threatened suicide many times, although hadn't self-mutilated (apparently, many BPD sufferers resort to "cutting", which she had never done). Her frequent and inappropriate displays of anger were obvious, as well as the unstable relationships, and the feelings of unreality and paranoia could be found in her expression of dismay at people "not liking her", when those very same people told me later that they had loved her because she was kind to them! As far as her feelings of abandonment went, I'm pretty certain that her declarations to us that she was finished with us forever, followed by a phone call less than a week later to say that she missed us, was proof of that.

Even the calm behaviour that we had witnessed during the time that she came home to live with us after breaking up with Keith for good was a manifestation of BPD, as sufferers will often go through periods of "reasonableness" before returning to their usual behaviour (which explains her inability to live peacefully with Brandon after almost a year of calm when she lived with us).

I wish that I had sought out the books that I have read recently at the time that Dr. Andrews told me about his suspicions of her disorder. At the time, I was content with what I had read on the Internet, but was also dismayed to find that there was very little treatment for her problem. I hoped that, eventually, she would seek help and get a proper diagnosis, confirmed by a psychiatrist, and we could go from there.

Reference: Dr. Robert O. Friedel, Borderline Personality Disorder Demystified - an Essential Guide for Understanding and Living with BPD, Da Capo Press, 2004.

Amy Goes To Court

The day finally arrived when Amy had to go to court to answer to the charges of shoplifting and impersonation of her sister. Mr. Latimer was still her attorney, and we were very grateful, as he hadn't been paid anything by her (or us) since the previous winter. Ed and I were in a position of owning two houses at this time (we had never managed to sell our first house when moving to the new one, as a recession had arrived in North America by the fall of 2009 and the housing market was badly hit. Tenants were paying the mortgage for us at that time!) and chiropractic fees had been removed from health care. I was working full-time for a family physician by now, to help with the family finances, and Ed was continuing with his two jobs. However, there was nothing left over to pay the legal fees of our troubled and mostly unemployed daughter.

We picked Amy up and drove her to court. She was once again not ready, although very smartly dressed, when we arrived to pick her up, and I was upset with her for making us late. She then became furious with me, and the fight was on all the way to the courthouse. It continued as we waited outside the courtroom for Mr. Latimer, and only ended when he told Amy to put away her coffee cup and come and talk to him in private.

We were eventually ushered into the courtroom and had to sit through another case before Amy's was heard. The judge was a very stern man and had the previous offender in tears by the time he was done. (She was a middle-aged woman who had abused her company's trust in her by stealing from them in order to supplement her family income when her husband became sick). We were very nervous for Amy!

The prosecutor outlined Amy's offences and I was sure that she didn't stand a chance. I was so worried that she would be sentenced and would finally end up in jail, the thing that I most dreaded for her as I was sure it would mean the end of her life. She definitely sounded like a hardened criminal when the prosecutor spoke about her. Mr. Latimer then stood up and we began to feel a little more confidence in his case. He stated that we were in the courtroom, showing our support for our daughter, and he emphatically insisted that she was a reformed person since the time of the commission of her offences. He told the judge that she had completed three months of rehab and was enrolled in hairdressing school, a career that could be very promising for her. At the time, my stomach lurched, as I knew that she had been kicked out of rehab and was no longer attending school. However, I felt that Mr. Latimer knew what he was doing and I didn't want to make a scene.

Well, the judge decided that he would once again put off the case before sentencing. It was remanded to three more months away, and we were all again put through the agony of waiting and not knowing what was going to happen to Amy.

The day finally arrived for the final trial and sentencing. We made sure she got to court on time, although she was very surly and difficult to deal with on the day (probably because of her anxiety). Mr. Latimer arrived late, as he was involved in a high-profile criminal case. However, once there, he continued to build a good case for her. Yes, she was guilty of shoplifting and impersonating her sister but, at the time, she was a crystal meth addict and had been living with a self-professed criminal. She had since gone to a rehab facility for three months and was attending college for hairdressing. She was repentant of her past, and her parents were supporting her in court.

The prosecution felt that she should go to jail, mostly for the imperson-ation of her sister. Amy had told us, prior to going into the courtroom, that if she received a jail sentence, she was planning to "bolt" from the courtroom. Alarmed, I had replied that that was not a good idea. They always had sheriffs in the room, and she wouldn't get very far once the city police were alerted. Her sentence would then probably be lengthened.

While the prosecutor delivered her speech, Amy sobbed quietly in the docket. The judge, a kind-looking middle-aged woman whom Mr. Latimer had expressly requested for her trial, looked over at her several times and listened attentively. When it was his turn, Mr. Latimer expounded on Amy's deep regret of her actions and efforts to rebuild her life, supported by her family. The sheriffs had entered the room before the final sum-mation and it was obvious that they were expecting a guilty verdict.

And guilty it was! However, the judge said that she saw remorse on Amy's face and in her behaviour, and in her efforts to build a new, constructive life for herself. Her stay in a rehab facility and her current attendance at hairdressing school spoke well for her, and it was obvious that she had the support of her family, who would try to keep her on the straight and narrow.

Her sentence was one year's probation. She was to visit a probation officer monthly, and receive a psychological assessment. I was very pleased about the latter, as I felt that she would finally get a confirmed diagnosis of BPD. She was also given a 9 p. m. curfew, told to stay out of bars and away from drug addicts and criminals, and to request permission from her probation officer before moving her living quarters.

When we left the court, we all hugged Mr. Latimer and each other. Amy was hugely relieved at having avoided a prison sentence, and we were happy for her. We thanked Mr. Latimer many times over, and I told Amy that she should get a job as soon as possible and start paying him for his services. She readily agreed.

She was also excited about starting a new life, drug-free and crime-free. She was going to become an exemplary member of society and live up to all of her probation restrictions. When we drove her home that night, it was a beautiful summer evening, and when I happened to glance at my watch and notice it was 8:55 p. m., I warned her that she was about to breach her curfew. She quickly said "good night", ran inside and up to her apartment.

We should have known that, as always happened with Amy, the good intentions were short-lived and the promises would only be fulfilled for a very short time. Trouble was again on the horizon, and it came in the form of her relationship with Rick. Although she knew he was a criminal, she continued to associate with him and many of the friends from her former life. Evidently, she hadn't learned anything from her brushes with the law. We should have known that. The lack of recognition of consequences of her actions was yet another manifestation of her disorder.

The Next Phase

Things were quiet for a little while. I visited Amy at her apartment a couple of times, and Ed and I even helped her move some furniture into the apartment one evening. She seemed happy to be there, and seemed to be complying with her curfew. She had even gone to see her probation officer once or twice and I thought that she had definitely turned over a new leaf. However, I was noticing a pattern in her life which was becoming a lot more prevalent than before. She was increasingly hard to get hold of, either by phone, text or on Facebook, and she also seemed to fail more and more to follow through on plans that were made.

On the night of her birthday, November 10th, we were supposed to meet her at Chianti's Restaurant for a dinner with her grandparents, sister and nephew. She had asked me if Rick could come too and, not wanting to spoil her birthday with an unpleasant scene, I had said yes.

Well, as were driving towards 17th Avenue, we got a phone call. It was Amy and she was crying hysterically. She said that she would not be attending her birthday dinner and, when we asked why, she wouldn't tell us. I gathered from some things she said that she was with Rick. They seemed to be having an argument and I could only assume that he was the reason for her sudden change of plans.

I tried very hard to convince her to come, even telling her that we would pick her up from wherever she was and bring her to the dinner. She refused, and eventually rang off, still sobbing.

We arrived at the restaurant feeling very glum, and proceeded to tell the family that she wouldn't be attending her birthday dinner. We all agreed to have dinner anyway, since we were already there.

Well, half an hour later, in walked Amy, with Rick in tow! We were very surprised to see them, but I was pleased. We didn't see much of Amy these days, and it was nice to know that she and Rick had somehow managed to put their argument behind them and join us for dinner.

During the course of the evening, her grandpa had one of his little "heart to heart" talks with her, telling her that she brought all of her problems on herself and had only herself to blame. As a victim of addiction himself at one time in his life, he knew the problems that it could cause, but he had beaten his demons and remained sober for the rest of his life. We didn't know at the time that Amy was back on drugs, but it seemed a reasonable conclusion, given her resumed relationship with Rick and the fact that, nine times out of ten, when you made plans with Amy, she failed to appear!

The next time that she let us down was on Christmas Day. Now, Amy loved Christmas, and she had always enjoyed family Christmas dinners. Our best memories of her were the Christmas at my brother's house with Brandon - how sweet she had been, and how beautiful and happy she had looked.

We looked forward to having her with us on that day in 2011, since we were hosting Christmas and my mother and brother from Toronto were there. It would be nice to have the whole family together again. Luc was going to be with us, and we anticipated a pleasant evening.

However, the arrival time of the family was 5 pm, and it came and went with no sign of Amy. I called her several times, and finally got hold of her.

"Where are you?" I asked her, sure I was sounding annoyed.

"I had an asthma attack this morning and was in the hospital," she replied. "But can I still come for dinner?"

I didn't know whether to believe her about the asthma. She had always had respiratory and sinus problems, probably due to her allergies, but nothing that had ever sent her to hospital. However, it was Christmas, and I didn't want to be the "mean mother".

"Sorry to hear about your asthma," I said. "Are you okay? Can you make it down here?"

"Yes", she replied, "Can I bring Rick?"

I said that she could, even though I was filled with trepidation at the thought of my Toronto family members meeting Rick. What would they think of a gang member (if, indeed, that was true)? He could be very nice when he was on his best behaviour, but would they approve of him? At the time, I was still trying to keep up appearances, but how could he be worse than any of her other boyfriends, or than Stephanie's ex-husband? I somewhat uncomfortably set two more places at the table and we all waited for Amy to show up - not for long, though. Since she was always late for everything, we decided to go ahead with our dinner when the turkey was ready!

As it turned out, I needn't have fretted about Rick fitting in with our family. Amy, of course, didn't show up and, in my usual manner, I was once again angry with her. During the latter years, I always experienced an ambivalence of feelings about her. I would be anxious to see her, then would dread her actually showing up (probably in case she embarrassed me or the family with her behaviour), then finally would be annoyed when she didn't show up. Doubtless other parents who have children who are addicts feel the same way, even more so if they have BPD! In her defense, though, she did post on her Facebook page, "Spent Christmas in the hospital with an asthma attack – thanks, Santa!"

Well, she didn't really spend the whole day in the hospital. She admitted to me later that she and Rick couldn't get a ride out to Okotoks and that's why she hadn't shown up that day. I was disappointed when I heard it, but thought that she and Rick had probably been celebrating Christmas in their own way. I felt that it was just one more manifestation of her narcissistic behaviour.

At first, I had sworn to myself that she would have to come and get her Christmas presents. There was no way I was going to take them to her! However, by mid-January, I was relenting and wanting to go and visit her again. I called her, and we made a date for the following Thursday, as that was my day off from the doctor's office.

I arrived at Amy's apartment at around noon and walked up to her door. I knocked on the door and waited. No response. I knocked again. Still no response. I knocked once more, then phoned her cellphone. I got her voicemail.

In frustration, I started back down the stairs, and got into my car. All of a sudden, my phone rang. It was Amy.

"Amy? Where are you?" I demanded. "I went to your apartment, like we arranged, and you're not there!"

"Which apartment?" she asked.

Dumbfounded, I answered, "Well, the apartment in Mount Royal, of course!"

"I haven't lived there in over a month," she replied.

"What?" I asked her. "When did you move?"

"About a month ago," she answered.

I obtained the address of her new apartment and went over there.

It was quite a nice little place, only about three blocks from the other one, and once again off 17th Avenue. She seemed to favour that area of Calgary.

When I asked for an explanation for the move, she said that her old apartment was too expensive, and that this new one was much more reasonable. I asked her whether she had informed her probation officer of the move, and she said that she hadn't. She also told me that the probation officer had been asking too many questions about the length of the programme that she had been in at Servants Anonymous, and whether she was still at Delmar College. She was sure that, if the officer found out that all was not as it had seemed to be at her trial, she would be marched straight off to jail. However, since attendance at both of these places had been conditions of her probation, and that informing the officer of any intended moves (before they took place, not afterwards!) was also a requirement, she was now in breach of her probation, so she could go to jail anyway. Just the fact that she had been attending bars and hanging out with the criminal element from her previous life was actually enough to breach the probation. It was obvious that she had no intentions of reforming. She had also not received a psychological assessment, and this bothered me, as I wanted to get her diagnosis of Borderline Personality Disorder confirmed by someone in the mental health field - not that I doubted Dr. Andrews' diagnosis. He had hit the nail on the head, in my opinion.

I wanted to wash my hands of her. I soon felt that someone who had been given a wonderful chance to start their life over and simply chose to carry on as she had before was not worth my care or attention. But she was my daughter, whom I loved very much and, as she had asked us in her lovely Christmas letter, I wasn't going to give up on her.

The Law Catches Up To Rick

Not long after that, I received a phone call from a Sheriff Robert Whiteside, who belonged to a law enforcement agency tasked with tracking down criminals who have eluded arrest or have breached their probation. However, he wasn't looking for Amy. He was looking for Rick.

I asked him why, and he said that Rick had been involved in a kidnapping and extortion case, and that they wanted us to help the police bring him in. He asked if I knew where he was and could give them an address. I hadn't actually seen Rick since Amy's birthday, and wasn't even sure she was still dating him, as they had a constant on-again, off-again relationship and she certainly wasn't living with him. She had got her apartment on her own and had told us that she couldn't live with him; he was too difficult. (A bit of the pot calling the kettle black, I think!)

Anyway, Sheriff Whiteside told me that just being around Rick was dangerous for Amy, as some day someone would come looking for him to settle a score, and she might be in the way. Little did I know how prophetic his words would be!

At the time, I had no idea where Rick was living, so told Sheriff Whiteside that I would help him if I could, but offered no information. He ended up having a phone conversation with Ed and actually told Ed that Rick wasn't really a gang member, he was just in a gang "in his own mind". So much for my daughter's pride in her boyfriend's "gangster" status! However, this information later proved to be wrong, as we were to find out.

That spring, Ed and I were involved in the production of a one-act play festival, hosted by our theatre group. One of the plays, in which our friends Fiorentina and Sean acted, actually won the regional festival and would then be advancing to the provincial festival. Everyone in the group was excited, and we all made plans to drive to Camrose for the festival weekend. It was mid-April, and we planned to drive up on the Friday afternoon for the big event.

The Thursday evening before the festival, we received a phone call from Amy.

"I've been evicted from my apartment, because Rick trashed the place!" she yelled hysterically. "They're going to throw all my stuff out on the street for the sheriff to come and pick up if I don't move it by Saturday afternoon! I don't have anyone to help me move – can you?"

We had always helped our kids move whenever they needed it, and Amy many times, but never on such short notice. We were going to Camrose (Ed was the producer of the play, and our truck was going to transport the set), and the words of Stephanie, Carla and my mother about not enabling Amy were ringing in my head.

"We can't, Amy," I replied. "We have to go to Camrose this weekend for a play festival."

"But all my stuff will be seized by the sheriff, if I don't move out on Saturday!" she yelled at me.

"Sorry, but we're going away, " I answered firmly. "You'll have to find someone else to help you move this time."

She promptly hung up the phone on me, only to call back again a few minutes later to reiterate her request that we drop everything and help her move.

"Can't Rick help you, if it's his fault?" I asked.

"We're fighting, and I hate him!" she replied.

"Well, don't you have any other friends who can help you?" I demanded.

"No, I don't!" she cried.

"Well, I'm sorry, but we're going to Camrose."

"Then why don't you f*** off to Camrose?" was her answer. "I'm just going to kill myself!"

And she hung up. I immediately regretted my firmness and determination not to give in! Horrified, I tried to call her back again. No answer. I tried several times, but she refused to pick up the phone. I tried texting her, but she still wouldn't answer. What if she really meant what she had said? In a panic, I did what I had done when she was a teenager, and called my mother-in-law to see if she could help.

My mother-in-law tried, then called me back to tell me that Amy had also hung up on her and refused to answer the phone again. I had one more card up my sleeve which I thought I could use, and called my friend Fiorentina, the actress. She had worked in social work in the past, and understood some things about rebellious young people, and also about

BPD. She had previously met and worked with Amy in one of our plays, and really loved her.

"I'll try talking to her," she told me. "But, if I can't get through to her, you might want to call the police if she's threatening suicide."

"I will!" I replied. "I don't know whether to believe that she'll go through with it, or whether she's just bluffing to get us to do what she wants."

"That's a chance you probably shouldn't take. Are you willing to go ahead and call the police?"

"Yes, I am," I answered.

So Fiorentina tried to contact Amy, and then phoned and told me that she wouldn't even answer her phone. I dialed 911.

I had only been to Amy's new apartment once, so I had great difficulty giving the police the address. At first I gave them the wrong address, then Ed went on the Internet and I identified the apartment building from what I saw on the computer screen.

The police called me about half an hour later. They had knocked on Amy's door and entered her apartment, much to her dismay. I could hear her screaming at them in the background, as one of the young policemen remonstrated with her. Apparently, she had been asleep, and that's why she wouldn't answer the phone. So much for committing suicide!

She was furious with me for daring to call the police on her. I could hear the young officer telling her in the background,

"Amy, your mom was worried about you. That's why she called us."

I heard the string of expletives that followed this. The policemen informed us that they would be taking her to hospital for a psychiatric assessment (standard procedure after a suicide threat), which made her even angrier, as she had to pack to move. I asked them not to, and said that we would go by the next morning and help her at least pack, although we couldn't help with the actual move.

However, they did follow procedure and take her to the hospital, and I found a string of furious texts on my phone the next morning calling me every name under the sun. Ed phoned her after that and informed her that we would not be helping anyone to move who called her mother such abusive names.

We then got in the truck and drove to Camrose, although I have to admit that I fretted the entire way there! Fiorentina rode in the truck with us, and she told me that we had done the right thing.

Camrose was a huge success, with our theatre group winning the provincial title, thanks to Fiorentina and Sean. We celebrated late into the night and then finally turned in during the wee hours of the morning. We drove home triumphantly the next day and then, as was so often the case with our busy lives in those days, attended a rehearsal of the new musical play our group was involved in. I had a role in the play, and Ed was part of the band that would be playing the songs.

Halfway through rehearsal, I was sitting with my fellow actor (we played husband and wife) when my cellphone went off.

I got up to answer it and quickly realized it was Amy,

"I tried to get someone else to move me", she said, "but they left when they realized that they wouldn't have any help with the heavy furniture. Can you guys help me?"

"You mean the sheriff didn't seize your things when you didn't move out yesterday?" I asked.

"No," she replied innocently, evidently forgetting the story she had told me on Thursday night.

"Can you wait till we're finished with rehearsal?" I asked her.

"Yes," she replied.

I returned to my seat beside my fellow actor.

"Everything okay?" he inquired, seeing the glum look on my face.

"No!" I replied, my anger with Amy suddenly surfacing. "We have to go and help our daughter move out of her apartment, right after we're done here. And we hardly got any sleep last night in Camrose. We're both exhausted!"

On seeing his sympathetic look, I added,

"We have a delinquent daughter. She hangs out with criminals and gets herself evicted from her apartments every few months!"

I realized when he looked uncomfortable and didn't reply that I had elaborated too much, so apologized quickly to him. I had become so used to Amy's situations that I sometimes didn't realize the inappropriateness of telling people who didn't know her the grim truth.

Well, we did as we had promised and went to her apartment after the rehearsal. Fiorentina felt sorry for us, feeling obligated to help Amy move after she had been so abusive to us.

When we arrived there, Amy was still in the process of packing and greeted us cheerily. She had a girlfriend who was supposedly helping her, but the girlfriend kept receiving phone calls, disappearing in a car with different fellows, and then returning about half an hour later and sitting to watch us work. Amy didn't tell me what she was up to, but I had my suspicions.

I asked Amy where she was going to live after this. She told me that she would move in with Rick for a short time, until she could find another place to live. She seemed nervous at the prospect of living with him, as she said that they had been fighting a lot and he had been beating her again. She showed me some "bruises" on her arms, but I really couldn't see anything. The apartment also didn't seem to be "trashed", as she had told me on the phone the other night. This was once again one of those situations where the truth didn't measure up to what she had told us. Actually, Stephanie had once had to go and "rescue" her from Rick's apartment when they had been having a fight (we had company over that night and couldn't leave) and had been surprised to see no bruises on Amy's face, in spite of Amy having told her that Rick had kicked and punched her. Stephanie did say, however, that she had a few red marks and scratches on her body, but nothing on her face. Amy had always exaggerated things, as we knew from when she had been a young child, but it always surprised me how she couldn't figure out that people might call her on her stories! The lack of connection to reality may have been a manifestation of her BPD.

Anyway, we continued to pack up her things and put them into our truck. I stayed indoors with her and Ed remained outside, organizing the truck. When Amy and I talked about Rick, the discussion escalated into an argument when I told her that she should go to a shelter, rather than to his house. She started calling me names again and, when I threatened to quit helping her and return home, she did at least have the sense to back down. She also promised never to threaten suicide again, at risk of having the police called!

As we were loading up the final haul of furniture and possessions, Amy looked down the alley and suddenly said,

"Well, look who decided to show up!"

I looked in the direction she was pointing, but saw nobody.

"Who?" I asked.

"Rick!" she replied. I looked a second time, but again saw nobody. He must have been hiding behind a tree, or a bush.

"Has he come to help?" I inquired.

"I guess so," she answered. "Who would have thought it?"

Apparently, Rick was by now afraid of us, or of our disapproval of him, and wouldn't show his face, but he had had a change of heart about helping her with her move and, after we left, he did help her with the final load.

So she moved in with him for about a month and all seemed to be going reasonably well, although there was one occasion when she called me and asked me to pick her up, because they were fighting again. I obliged, and was rather shocked at the shabby appearance of the hallway of the apartment building where they were living. I never actually saw the apartment itself.

It was not long after that incident that she called to tell us that Rick had been arrested by the police and was in jail. It looked as though Sheriff Whiteside had caught up with him, after all!

Ami Jane Marshall - Amy's 'alter ego'

Amy Reconnects With Mark

Amy continued to live in Rick's apartment for a short time and then, suddenly, got evicted. I never found out exactly what happened, but it had something to do with the landlord and an incident with a "fake" gun! She never elaborated on the details, but evidently she had offended the landlord enough for him to request her to vacate the premises. She also had probably not paid him any rent as, with Rick in jail, she had nobody to support her and pay her way.

She once again asked to move back home with us and, mindful of our determination to not enable her, we said no. We did offer to help her pay the rent for a couple of months, if she would find another place to live and get a paying job.

As the days marched on and she still didn't have a permanent place to live (she was mostly "couch-surfing" with friends), she decided to go back to go-go dancing and was eventually able to move in with a friend, an artist who painted bizarre pictures of beautiful women, but with half of their faces shown as skulls, and bones protruding through their skin on various limbs. (We later found out that he was a heroin addict, who had several young women living with him. I believed at the time that he was just a kind person who helped homeless girls by providing them shelter. Once again, I was so naïve!)

We were relieved that Rick had gone to jail and thought, as Sheriff Whiteside had told us, that he would be there for a very long time. We advised Amy not to contact him, or have anything to do with him, and she seemed to be content not to.

During the time that she lived at the artist's apartment, one of her roommates (a friend named Talisa who was also a go-go dancer and probably invited her to move there in the first place) said that she had noticed a big change in Amy that summer. The main reason can be attributed to Mark – the Mark from Kelowna (whom she had gone to visit two years before), not her old boyfriend, Mark. Apparently, they had kept in touch after she came back to Calgary and he had always been very supportive of her. In fact, he moved back to Calgary not long after she phoned him to tell him that she had been evicted and had nowhere to go. However, she also appeared to be going through another period of calm (as BPD sufferers often do), and this may have explained the change in her behaviour noted by her friends.

Mark was kind to Amy. He later told me that he had fallen in love with her the very first time he met her and he always left her free to do whatever she wanted. He never argued with her, or made any demands on her, and treated her with the kindness and care that we now know sufferers of Borderline Personality Disorder need. They have to be handled with gentleness, not toughness and severity. I have only read books on the disorder since losing Amy, mostly because I hadn't been aware of any books that had been written to help the lay person understand its complexities. I have many regrets about not reading books on the subject when she was still alive but, at the time, we were always hopeful that she would receive a proper assessment and diagnosis, and understanding would flow from that.

Mark's gentle treatment of her seemed to enable her to flourish, and she even hung on to her job that summer. He apparently had some type of work as a courier and, although they didn't live together, they spent a lot of time together. Her happiness and more stable mood seemed evident to everyone who knew her.

The only fly in the ointment was that Rick was still writing to her from jail, accusing her of having another boyfriend (she always denied to him, and even to me, that Mark was her boyfriend) and threatening to harm her when he got out. We had been assured that he would not get out, so we didn't spend too much time worrying about it.

In June of that year, I went to Hawaii with my mum for our respective milestone birthdays. It was a wonderful holiday in an earthly paradise, and Mum and I returned very much refreshed. I had bought souvenirs for all of my family members and gave them out on my return. However, contacting Amy was, as always, difficult, and I hung on to the pretty necklace I had bought her for about a month.

I finally managed to reach her, and we arranged to go for lunch at Chinook Centre in Calgary the following day.

As usual, as I was driving in to the city that day, I called Amy and got no reply the first three times. I texted her when I arrived at another mall a little further south of Chinook, but again got no reply.

Finally, as I was driving towards my destination, my phone rang. I picked it up. (This happened prior to the Distracted Driver's law, which prohibits cellphone use while driving!) It was Amy.

"Amy!" I said in a relieved tone. "Aren't we meeting for lunch?"

"I don't know," she replied. "Mark and I have a lot of errands and stuff to do."

"But, Amy," I said. "I'm driving to Chinook to meet you, and I really want to see you. Besides, I have a present for you from Hawaii."

I heard some muffled conversation and swear words in the background and then she came back on the phone.

"We're not ready to go out", she insisted. "We still have to leave the house and drive there!"

"I'll come and pick you up. Give me your address," I answered her.

That elicited more swear words and muffled conversation. Finally, I started telling her how much I missed her and wanted to see her. It was true – I hadn't seen her since the day we moved her out of Rick's apartment, and I wanted to spend some time with her.

She finally reluctantly agreed, and I pulled into the parking lot of Chinook Centre and made my way to the food court. I bought some Greek food and found a table, reading a magazine as I waited for her.

She breezed in about twenty minutes later. She looked beautiful that day! She had once again dyed her hair brown, and it was brushed and shining. Her makeup wasn't smudged, as it so often was, and her clothes were clean and stylish. I was so impressed with the change in her, as opposed to when I had last seen her, that I told her at once that I thought she looked great.

We had a lovely lunch, which I paid for. I gave her the gift, and she immediately put in on. We chatted about her life, work and Mark. She did mention Rick, and said that he was still in jail, to which I expressed relief. I told her not to have any contact with him, and she agreed that she didn't want to.

Mark phoned her several times during our lunch, and I urged her to invite him along. He repeatedly refused, and seemed to want her to wrap up our lunch so that they could go and do the "errands and stuff" that she had told me about. We eventually got up to leave, and he again phoned to insist that she meet him outside in the parking lot immediately.

"Yes, yes, I'll be there in a minute!" she told him loudly. "I haven't finished visiting with my mum."

We took the escalator down to the main floor of the mall and then wended our way out into the parking lot. As we were walking, I saw a black SUV come towards us and eventually recognized Mark as the driver. He stopped for Amy, and she turned and gave me a big hug.

"Thanks for lunch, Mum! Love you!" she said.

I hugged her back, told her I loved her too and then greeted Mark, admonishing him for not joining us for lunch. (He later told me that he was high on drugs that day, and was ashamed for me to see him that way.)

I waved at the vehicle as they drove away, and my daughter waved back. I for the first time in a long time felt some inner peace that she had finally found her way in life. Of course, I was wrong, as I so often was when it came to Amy!

Note: Mark never seemed to go to work, although he was still awaiting his payment for the "job" he did. At the time, I thought he had some type of work as a courier, but didn't find out what he really did until much later – he was involved in the drug business, and also with identity theft and credit card fraud, much as Amy had been when she was with Keith.

The Storm Approaches

Another month went by and Amy kept in touch, mostly by phone or Facebook post. Meanwhile, I had quit my job in the medical office by the end of July and found a less stressful post working in a salon and spa. I was again doing reception, and the women I worked with were mostly young and very friendly. I knew a lot of the clientele from living so many years in Okotoks and, in fact, reconnected with several women whose children had attended pre-school and kindergarten with ours.

Ed was still working full-time in his practice and continuing on Okotoks Town Council. Stephanie was pursuing her studies, now taking kinesiology after completing her psychology degree. Michael was up in Edmonton, having finished a diploma in music and then joining a heavy metal band which was having some success in performing and recording.

All seemed well with the world. Amy was, to the best of our knowledge, still working at her job and living at the artist's apartment – not an ideal situation, but at least she had a roof over her head.

Sometimes, Amy would come for dinner at our house with Stephanie. One day in July, she arrived with Steph and her friend, Patricia, who had gone to school with the girls and was now living in Edmonton. I was somewhat intimidated about cooking dinner for Patricia, as she was a chef by trade, but she laughed and told me that it was great to have someone else do the cooking for a change! Dinner started out well, but rapidly deteriorated.

Amy was upset about one of her friends, a petty criminal who had attempted to rob a house and subsequently died from a gunshot wound inflicted by a police officer arriving at the scene. Apparently, her friend had drawn a knife on the policeman, who acted in self-defense. She was mourning her friend, and we rather tactlessly reminded her that he was a gangster who basically got what he deserved when he threatened a police officer. Not only did I not make the comment, but I even expressed condolences, but maybe not in a very sincere tone. She then became furious with us and, as usual, her anger escalated from a score of 1 to 10 in less than a minute.

At some point during the argument, the fact that she probably had Borderline Personality Disorder came up and she immediately went downstairs to our computer to print off what she had read about the disorder on a website.

She returned a few minutes later, brandishing a piece of paper and reading out in a loud voice a paragraph in which the writer says that BPD is often triggered by "neglect and abuse in childhood".

"So you think that's why you have BPD?" I asked her.

"Yes," she replied. "It's because you neglected and abused me when I was a child!

I became incensed at the unfairness of this accusation and, although embarrassed that Patricia was witnessing the fight, told Amy that she was never neglected or abused, and challenged how she could say that to us. The current thinking regarding BPD is that, although it can be triggered by environmental factors, a genetic abnormality is necessary in order for it to develop. It can also develop in individuals who haven't been subjected to emotional or physical abuse during childhood.

Stephanie quickly grabbed Amy by the arm and took her out on to the deck to have a heart-to-heart discussion. They came back about ten minutes later and Amy announced that she was leaving. She had convinced Stephanie to drive her home, and we were left to finish dinner with Patricia. I apologized to Patricia for the commotion and expressed my embarrassment at the awful scene. She hastened to assure me that, "it wouldn't be the Sands household without drama"! I wasn't particularly comforted by these words. We never really had any drama unless Amy was on the scene, and most of our family dinners were pleasant affairs. Unfortunately, Patricia had been witness to many unpleasant episodes in the past.

Amy soon forgot about her anger with us, as usual, and we heard from her again a couple of weeks later. It was not good news. She told me that Rick would soon be getting out of jail, and she feared that he would "come after" her for seeing someone else while he was incarcerated. She wasn't officially dating Mark, but they were seeing a lot of each other and someone may have been informing Rick of this. Knowing that Rick had a temper, we all feared that he would make good on his threat! We told her to stay as far away from him as she could, and she agreed that she intended to. I felt extremely let down by the legal system, however, as we had been assured by Sheriff Whiteside that Rick was going away for a long time. Instead of which, when he went to court, his lawyer pinned the whole thing on his now deceased partner in crime and Rick was going to be released, due to "time served".

During the last week of August, Amy texted me and asked me whether she could come and stay with us for a few days. She said that the air in her apartment was bad and was causing her asthma to act up. (She suspected mould in the building). She had missed a lot of workdays due to the asthma and her boss was now asking for a note from her family doctor. She also said that she was very tired and needed to rest for a few days. I suspected also that Rick's approaching release from jail and Mark's desire to protect her from Rick had something to do with it.

My initial instinct was to say no. I felt that she was probably just working her way back to asking to move in with us again. We had Michael coming home for the long weekend, and our grandson coming for a sleepover, so I didn't think I would have a spare room for her, and I started to text her that she couldn't come. Upon reflection, though, I realized that it might be good for her to be out of Calgary on the day that Rick was released. I re-read the text she had sent me, and realized that she was only asking for two days (Monday to Wednesday), as she was expected back at work on the Thursday evening. I quickly erased my text that denied her request and typed out, "Yes, you can come. Just let me know what time you'll be arriving." I'm so glad I made that decision.

Mark phoned me the day before she was due to come, to let me know her expected arrival time, and to ask me to make an appointment for her with Dr. Andrews. He admitted that he was worried about Rick being on the hunt for her, and I urged him to take her back to B. C. with him, to get her out of harm's way. He replied that he didn't have any money, but was waiting for a big payout from a job he had done and would then take her back to his parents' house. I told him that I would front him the gas money, if he would just take her away immediately, but he seemed hesitant.

I called Dr. Andrews' office, but was told by the nurse that he was booked up for the entire week and that Amy would have to go to our local emergency clinic. I was assured that she would get an appropriate note there, and so didn't try to insist on an appointment.

She arrived on the Monday evening, and she looked terrible! What a change from only a month ago, when I had met her at Chinook Centre. Her hair was once again blond, but it was now messy and unbrushed.

Her makeup was smeared around her eyes, which wasn't all that out of the ordinary, but her face had a generally "hard" look about it that I really couldn't define. I immediately put it down to drug use, but she assured me that she had stopped using drugs and that it was her asthma that was making her look haggard. (However, a very good friend of hers told us recently that Rick had got her started on heroin just before he went to jail, and this may have accounted for the hardened look.) She informed me that the last doctor she had seen had suggested that she might have C.O.P.D. (Chronic Obstructive Pulmonary Disease), which was a very serious respiratory illness. I immediately felt guilty that I had suspected her of continued drug use when she was telling me that she was sick.

Mark came by to see her the next day, and I expected that he would have taken her to the emergency clinic for her doctor's note. Instead, they spent the afternoon in the basement and going for walks in the neighbourhood. Now, Ed and I were hosting a meeting of the theatre group's executive that evening, and I wasn't anxious to have Amy around when the members started showing up at our house. Once again, my ambivalence about her appearance and her unpredictable behaviour reared its ugly head, and I urged her to go to the clinic before we started the meeting. She replied that she could go the next day, but I insisted that she go that evening.

"Why are you always trying to get rid of me?" she demanded angrily.

"I'm not!" I replied, feeling guilty, as that's exactly what I was trying to do. "But you need to get that note as soon as possible, so that you can have it in time to go back to work on Thursday."

She reluctantly conceded, and she and Mark left before the first board member appeared. Later in the evening, I told the executive that Amy had returned for a couple of days and that she "looked like hell" when she showed up on our doorstep. Fiorentina, who was on the board and had recently separated from her husband that summer, showed great concern for Amy and asked how she was doing. I explained that she was home for some respite from the bad air in her apartment, and possibly to get away from Rick. Fiorentina seemed pleased that we had done the right thing in letting her come home.

Amy reappeared with Mark before the meeting was over, this time with her hair combed and looking a little less unkempt. I breathed a sigh of relief (still concerned about appearances!). Some of the board members who knew her from her involvement in previous productions inquired about her health, and Fiorentina talked to her about her precarious situation with Rick. She also confided her own situation to Amy, and Amy was actually moved to tears for Fiorentina's unhappiness. Fiorentina told me later that she had thought Amy was crying because she was afraid of Rick coming after her (and, in fact, she had expressed deep anxiety over it), but Amy hastened to assure her, "No, I'm crying for you."

Fiorentina was very touched, and told me the next day that on the drive home she had had a horrible gut feeling that she should take Amy back to her house to stay with her for a few days, as she feared something bad was going to happen to her. I told her that she wouldn't have been happy having another "child" (on top of her own two little girls) to add to her household, as Amy wouldn't help her with the cooking and cleaning in spite of protestations of help offered! If only I had listened to Fiorentina, or to my own gut feeling that I should keep her in Okotoks for a while, just until Mark could take her away to B. C.

Fiorentina also later told me that she and Amy had exchanged some text messages the following day, in which she asked Amy whether she wanted to come back to live with us once again. She actually copied the texts to me, so that I could read them myself. Amy had replied that "it was what she wanted, but it was up to them" (us). Would we have allowed her to come back and live with us once more? Probably not, in view of the way things had gone before and because of our promise to ourselves and to our family to no longer enable her. However, would that have saved her from what was coming? We will never know.

Regrets don't do any good in life. You can beat yourself up over the things you could have done, or should have done, but it won't change what happens. We couldn't have foreseen the storm that was coming, but I still wish that we could have battened down the hatches beforehand! If so many things had been different up till then, perhaps the outcome would have changed, but I think that fate hands us the cards that we are dealt and nothing will change the way things come to pass.

The following day, I had a nice dinner with Amy and Mark, who had reappeared that afternoon. They went for a walk after supper, and when they returned, went down to the bedroom in the basement so that she could work on my sewing machine, which was stored there. She still loved sewing and found it a very relaxing pastime. She seemed to be looking better, and I thought she appeared more rested.

I went down there just before bed, and told her that Mark shouldn't stay over (in case that's what they were thinking!), as he was still there, lounging on the bed, watching her sew. She told me that she might return to Calgary that night, but I assured her she was welcome to stay the night, for which she thanked me. I gave her a hug and a kiss, and said good night to her. Little did I know that I would never see her alive again.

Source unknown, 2010.
The cover artwork by Lawrence Stilwell is based on this image.

The Worst Day Of Our Lives

On Thursday, I returned home from work, half expecting to find Amy still in the basement and to have to drive her back to Calgary for work, as I had promised. However, she had already left, and Ed later told me that Mark had driven her back. Ed always worked late on Thursdays and he told me that he had given Amy a hug and kiss goodbye and warned her to stay as far away from Rick as possible. He told me that she had assured him she would, and that she was afraid of Rick and what he might do.

When I had returned home from work, I noticed that my bathroom scale was missing. Amy had told us not long before that she no longer stole things but I, knowing her obsession with her weight and her some-times nimble fingers in the past when it came to "borrowing" my makeup and such, immediately thought she had either helped herself to it, or had taken it down to the basement and left it there. It was nowhere to be found in the house, so I texted her and asked her what had happened to it. She replied that she knew nothing about it and, when she started to sound defensive, I didn't press the issue. She then went on to say,

"Thank you for lettering (sic) me stay at your house to rest. I love you"

I was very touched by that and responded back that she was welcome, and that I loved her, too. I'm so grateful that I had the chance to text those words to her, especially after practically accusing her of stealing something as unimportant as a bathroom scale! (I later found out who had taken it and was annoyed at that person for not letting me know.) Her last text gave me a little peace of mind during what was to follow, and was actually used as part of the eulogy given by a pastor friend of ours at her funeral.

Mark called during the evening, and I (ever persistent) asked him about the bathroom scale. He knew nothing about it, and said he certainly hadn't seen Amy with it. He then went on to thank me for letting her rest at our house, and I asked him whether she was feeling better. He replied that he thought she was and that the short stay with us had done her good.

That night, just before we went to bed, I attempted to take a wooden tray down from a cupboard above the fridge in the kitchen and pulled it out too quickly. It came crashing down from the cupboard, striking the glass pantry door next to it and smashing the door. To this day, I've always believed that it was a bad omen of what was to come and, although many people have reassured me that it was just coincidence, I've never been able to shake that belief.

The morning of Friday, August 31st was sunny and beautiful, with a gorgeous long weekend ahead promised by the weatherman. I showered and dressed and decided to put the radio on to hear the news.

The first thing I heard was that a woman had been shot in the Dover area, and that a man had run from the house, screaming, "Oh my God, he killed her!"

My immediate thought was, "It's Rick! He got Amy, just like he said he would. And that was Mark running from the house."

But then I dismissed the thought, remembering that a man had killed his wife in the Forest Lawn area (adjacent to Dover) only the week before, and I assumed that this was just another such domestic case.

I went to work early, to get my hair done before starting my afternoon shift. The stylist and I chatted and, while I was waiting for the colour to set on my hair, I was told that there was a phone call for me. Now, I should mention that August of 2012 was a month of "blue moon", when there are two full moons in one calendar month. It was the week of the second full moon, and my boss had commented that all kinds of unusual things had been happening at the salon, mostly involving emotional clients crying over their hair, and one lady calling from vacation in the southern States to arrange an appointment because she wasn't happy with her haircut from the week before. The salon is famous for its excellent work and very talented hair stylists, but that week the "weirdos" were all calling in!

I picked up the phone with trepidation (I wasn't even supposed to start my shift until one p. m. and it was only 11:30. Who was calling me there?). It was Ed.

"Do you have Mark's phone number?" he asked me.

"No, not on me, I replied, "but it should be on the call display at home. He called last night."

"I'm not at home," he said.

"Well, you can check it when you go home for lunch," I told him, but I was getting a weird, uncomfortable feeling throughout my body. The story I had heard on the news was flashing through my mind. Afraid to hear the answer, I asked him,

"Does this have anything to do with that shooting in Calgary?"

"I'll tell you later," he said.

"Tell me now!" I replied urgently. "What's going on?"

"I had a phone call from 'Good Rick'," he answered hesitantly. (We had started referring to the two "Ricks" in Amy's life as "Good" and "Bad", delineating their status with the law and their influence on Amy). "He says something's going on. It's on Facebook, and he told me to call the police, but they won't tell me anything."

The feeling of dread deepened in my stomach, but I felt that we would have been the first to know if something had happened to our daughter so, as I had done in the morning when I heard the news, I let my brain rule out my gut feeling. This is something I've never done since – there's a reason for those scary intuitions, as I was to find out.

After I hung up the phone, I returned to the hairdresser's chair and told her what had happened. She reiterated that if anything had happened to Amy, we would already have been contacted by the police. I agreed with her, and dismissed the whole thing as a tempest in a teapot, but I still couldn't shake that bad feeling.

Ten minutes later, my young co-worker, Andrea, appeared at the hairdressing station in tears. She asked me whether I could start work early, as her dog, who had been sick all night, was at the vet and had to be put down. I told her that I would rush home and change for work as soon as the stylist was finished with my hair.

When I was done, I walked by the front desk and saw her crying heartbrokenly. I went to the staff room and told one of the stylists that I didn't think that Andrea would last out until I got back. She obliged by going to the desk and comforting her, telling her to go home.

I went home, changed, packed a sandwich and came back to work. My boss was sitting at the desk, answering the phone while there was no official receptionist. She informed me that Andrea had gone to stay with her dog during his last moments.

I sat down, we chatted for a few minutes and then I began my shift. Around 2:30 p. m., Ed suddenly appeared at the door. He walked in and, with a horrible sinking feeling, I knew what he had come for. I looked questioningly up at him and he nodded. My feeling of dread from the morning increased tenfold.

"It's her?" I asked.

He didn't have to reply. I knew it was Amy. Our gorgeous, vibrant but troubled daughter was gone! My world came crashing down around me.

"What's going on?" my boss asked, a puzzled look on her face.

"That shooting in Calgary? Did you hear about it on the news?" I stuttered.

"No," she replied.

"My daughter . . ." was all I could get out. Horrified, she grabbed my hand, tears in her eyes, then told me to leave and take as much time as I needed. We ran out of the salon.

When we got outside, grief, shock, horror, disbelief, guilt, and regret all washed over us in waves. We clung to each other for a long time, sobbing, then finally collected ourselves and fell to the horrible task of informing our families. We got into Ed's truck and called our parents, siblings and close friends. Ed had been told to come to the police station in northwest Calgary to talk to some detectives and we began the long drive through busy long-weekend traffic, with everyone trying to get out of town for the last long break of the summer. Stephanie was to meet us there.

By an impulsive and thoughtless act, our beautiful daughter had been taken away from us, just at the time that we believed her life seemed to be turning around and there was new hope for her future.

She was only 27.

OKOTOKS
Western Wheel

WEDNESDAY, SEPTEMBER 5, 2012 · VOL. 34 NO. 4 · WWW.WESTERNWHEEL.COM · YOUR COMMUNITY NEWSPAPER · FIRST IN THE FOOTHILLS

Daughter of local councillor killed in Calgary

By Darlene Casten
Assistant Editor

Okotoks Coun. Ed Sands said the news his daughter was likely shot and killed at a home with had ties to organized crime was not a surprise, but the death is still devastating to the family.

Sands said his daughter Amy, also known as AmiJane Marshall, had been struggling with addiction problems for a number of years and they escalated in the past four years

with the Calgary Police Service said a number of people have been interviewed, but a suspect has not yet been identified in Amy's death.

Neighbours said the house has been a constant problem for almost a year with people coming and going from a garage in the backyard at all hours of the night.

A woman, who asked to only be identified as Joyce, said the police had been to the house a number of times. She heard gunfire at around 6:30 a.m. on Friday and then saw a

Family says
shooting
victim was
caught in

CROSSFIRE

Western Wheel, Sept. 5, 2012
Calgary Sun, Sept. 2, 2012
Calgary Herald, Sept. 3, 2012

B2 Monday, September 3, 2012   CITY & REGION   Breaking news at calgaryherald.com

Victim was daughter of councillor

Okotoks family shocked by 'drug home' fatality

STEPHANE MASSINON
CALGARY HERALD

As a high school fine arts student, Amy Sands was a performer who could dazzle an audience. When she sang or acted she lit up the stage.

But in less than a decade, the daughter of Okotoks town councillor Ed Sands saw her life spiral into the grips of drug addiction. It ended the way her family had feared: dead at far too young an age.

Sands, who also went by the name AmiJane Marshall, has been identified by family as the victim of a homicide in Calgary, shot to death in a suspected drug home in Dover.

She was 27.

"She was a beautiful girl who had potential but chose the wrong path and ended up being at the wrong place at the wrong time," said her mother, Debbie Sands.

Debbie remembers her daughter's vibrant and free spirit.

"But she had some demons and problems. She hung around with a crowd that was not very safe."

The homicide unit is investigating her death and have not provided any updates on their investigation.

Police were first called to Dover Meadow Close at 6:30 a.m. Friday after neighbours phoned 911 to report gunshots. When police arrived, the body of the deceased woman was discovered.

"She had an ex-boyfriend who just got out of jail. When he was in jail he was always texting and harassing her and threatening things. For some reason, he got out on Wednesday and he kept calling her and she decided

to go and see him," Debbie said.

Debbie said the family encouraged Sands to seek treatment and she once went to rehab for three months.

"She wasn't ready. We tried many times to help her go there or to find other programs that would help. I don't think she ever reached the point where she felt she wanted to do it. It was always other people telling her she should," Debbie said.

Sands was born in Calgary but raised in Okotoks. Her father is a six-term councillor in the community south of Calgary.

He posted a Facebook message on the weekend thanking people for their support.

"Thank you to all our dear friends for your kind words and prayers on Amy's tragic passing. The support is truly appreciated," he wrote.

An autopsy is scheduled for early this week.

The family says they have not completed plans for her funeral and are

Amy Sands on her high school graduation day, left, a decade ago, and Sands more recently, right, after drugs took over her life.

waiting for the medical examiner to release the body.

The family heard the news of a fatal shooting on television Friday morning but initially did not realize the victim was Sands.

"We're all in shock and devastated, but I guess the one thing that we said (Friday) is that she's at peace now."

SMASSINON@CALGARYHERALD.COM

Aftermath

Along with Stephanie, we met with two detectives at the police station, and they told us that the deceased person was "allegedly" Amy Sands. They couldn't explain to our satisfaction why it had taken eight hours from the shooting (which had happened at 6:20 a. m.) for us to be informed, or why the first police officer that Ed had spoken to had refused to confirm or deny that she was the victim. In fact, it was only because Ed happened to have a Calgary policeman in his office, who had phoned them and insisted that he be told, that we found out when we did.

We weren't allowed to see her body, which is what I thought would happen upon our arrival there, as she was apparently "a crime scene". She had already been identified by "bad" Rick, and I became emotional at that point and told the officers that it was Rick who had killed her.

"She was terrified of him!" I told the officers.

"Actually, we took him into custody, and he's cooperating with us," one of them assured us. "He's not the one who did it, so we released him. He's quite distraught over it."

I didn't believe him. I was sure Rick had done it! And, if he didn't fire the fatal shot, he had arranged for it to happen.

The officers disagreed with me, and expressed their sincere condolences on our loss. I've never been satisfied with the way the whole thing was handled but, in defense of the Calgary police, I have to say that they're hampered by complex regulations and their hands are tied when it comes to investigations. The scenario of the police arriving at your door an hour after a violent crime or accident probably only happens in the movies. It's a sad comment, though, on the fact that news is often posted on Facebook long before the victim's family finds out. Another letdown in the way the legal system handles things these days.

We've made our peace with "bad" Rick, and he's no longer bad in our eyes. He was devastated by Amy's death, and still isn't over it. In our determination to blame someone, we at first requested him not to attend her funeral but, when he came to the viewing with one of Amy's friends, he was sobbing and remorseful, his arms full of her favourite roses. I couldn't help but forgive him, and our family did also. He loved her very much, and we couldn't prevent him from the closure of her funeral the following day (although there will never be any closure for us until the legal system has done its job, maybe not even then).

A man was arrested two days after her death, based on testimony provided to the police by Rick (and, as a gang member, which he definitely was, in spite of what Sheriff Whiteside told us, he put himself at risk by doing that). He was, in fact, stabbed by an unseen assailant about a month later, but thankfully was only wounded). This man had had an argument with Rick at the garage where Amy went to see him and had promised to return with a gun. Sure enough, he did come back and, after being startled by meeting Rick at the front door, ran around the back and shot through the garage car door. One of the shots he fired hit Amy in the neck, killing her instantly. She didn't suffer, which is the one thing we can be grateful for. The man is in jail awaiting trial at the time of writing, and we can only hope that the wheels of justice turn appropriately and that he's given a proper sentence for his crime.

Since her death, many people have reached out to us: people who have children who struggle with drugs; people who have struggled with drugs themselves and have decided to give up the lifestyle based on what happened to Amy; people who were bullied as children or who bullied others and, more recently, parents who have lost children suffering with Borderline Personality Disorder. Our other daughter, Stephanie, regressed greatly in her struggle at the time with her eating disorder after losing her sister, but that's her story and I will let her tell it. Our son, Mike, grieves the sister who was his nemesis in childhood, but then became very close to in later life, due to their shared interest in music. Little Luc grieves her also, and misses the aunty who always showed him much love and affection.

Because of Ed's position on Okotoks Town Council, the news media were interested in Amy's story and it was on TV and in the newspapers. A very kind reporter at the Calgary Herald interviewed us about Amy's life story and wrote a sympathetic article about her. We have never ceased to be amazed by the kindness and support we've received from the community and people in general, perhaps because of Ed's decision to share the details of Amy's troubles, rather than hide them, as I often tried to do.

I decided to follow his lead and give up my obsession with appearances, and I am now very honest and open about what her life was all about. She had her demons, but she was our angel in many respects, and we will continue to grieve her for the rest of our lives. She gave so much love to all of us, and had a huge and forgiving heart.

We will never know why she went to see Rick that morning. She went home after her shift at the night club, then "snuck" out the back way so that Mark and her roommates didn't see her. Mark had begged her not to meet Rick, who had been texting her constantly to come and see him. She took a cab, and apparently had a joyful reunion with Rick, of whom she had been claiming to be very afraid. Like a moth to the flame, she must have felt that irresistible draw to him, in spite of all the warnings from friends and family, and her own fears. I can only think that her sudden about-face was one facet of her mental illness, the need to indulge in high-risk behaviour.

There is now treatment available for people with Borderline Personality Disorder, once a diagnosis has been made. There are clinics in the Calgary area which specialize in Dialectical Behavioural Therapy (DBT), which is a relatively new therapy found to be very effective in helping the disorder. There are various other centres across Canada which also offer this therapy, and I urge anyone who suspects their child or loved one may have it to get a diagnosis. The treatment certainly helps sufferers and their families to understand and cope with it better.

We wish we could have understood it more at the time, and insisted that Amy seek treatment. However, one of the aspects of the disorder is denial by patients that there is anything wrong, so perhaps she wouldn't have. We will never know. Perhaps some day we will have the answers to the questions that we are seeking, perhaps never. We can only go on with our lives, honouring the memory of our lovely but troubled daughter and hoping that her life can serve as a helpful lesson to others with similar struggles.

We are keeping Amy's memory alive in a couple of different ways, besides the obvious ones of recognizing key dates in her life and of speaking to people about her.

Our theatre group has named a scholarship for her, and it is given to a student in the theatre programme at our local high school. It isn't given to the student who has the highest marks in theatre arts, but rather to the one who shows the most caring and concern for their fellow students, because that's what Amy excelled in. Despite her struggles, she always had a big heart and showed compassion to the person who felt like an outsider. It is heartwarming to shake hands with the young students who receive the award and to know that they are carrying on her legacy of kindness and caring, as well as her passion for the arts.

Each year, we hold a fundraiser in her name, right around the time of her birthday. It was originally organized by Stephanie, her friends and people who knew Amy through the entertainment industry – dancers, deejays, musicians. The proceeds from ticket sales and the silent auction go to a women's shelter in the Foothills area. We have managed to raise more money the second year than the first year, and we hope to continue to do so. It's something that we plan to do every year in November. If you are on Facebook, look for the "Amijane Funraiser", if it is something you would be interested in attending and live in the Calgary area. It's a fun night of music and dancing, as well as a great way to raise money for a good cause.

As Stephanie said, she doesn't want Amy's legacy to be that of a girl who was murdered in a garage, but rather of a girl who loved to dance and party with all of her friends. We try to keep that image of her in our minds at all times, and to celebrate the happy memories we have of her.

Post-script

December 2nd, 2014

It has been two years since we lost Amy, and we have gone through two bail hearings and one preliminary trial of the man who shot her. It has been very difficult hearing the details of that night over and over, and dealing with the courts and the legal system. Having to look the criminal in the face every time we went to court, and hearing his lawyer state that his client couldn't have done the shooting, was very hard on us. We relived that terrible morning every time we went to court, and many tears were shed.

During the preliminary trial in April, 2013, Rick was called to the witness stand and made the statement that he heard the gunshots at the back door ring out "immediately" after he closed the front door on the accused, who was holding a pellet gun in his hand.

The judge seized upon this evidence immediately and made it the turning-point of the whole case by saying that it was then clear that the accused had not committed the crime. His lawyer immediately jumped on that bandwagon, and insisted that it must have been the man who drove him to the crime scene who shot Amy, with a gun that was stowed in the truck. The fact that Rick had just taken speed and couldn't possibly have known whether the shot was immediate, or several seconds later, was completely ignored. In fact, other witnesses claimed that it was several seconds later.

The accused's girlfriend's evidence of his bragging about the murder, as well as the tattoo of a tear drop that he had done the very next day (signifying, in gang lore, that he had killed someone) was also ignored by the judge, who in fact refused to accept the testimony of the police gang expert about the tattoo, citing that he was not a "published author". I guess the fact that she was herself a published author was her reasoning behind her decision to dismiss the expert's testimony. Apparently, you can only be an expert on something if you have written a book or paper about it! This made no sense to us at the time, and still doesn't. This gave the defense more ammunition and, later that year, we were summoned to a meeting with the prosecution and told that they were considering lowering the charge to manslaughter, based on questions about the evidence (raised by the preliminary trial judge). We were outraged, especially on hearing of the possible downgrading of the sentence. The accused had clearly stated his intentions by text and phone call, on several separate occasions, to come back to the house with a gun and make sure that "everyone knew who he was" after that. He definitely had murder on his mind!

However, at that point, the defense lawyer wasn't willing to go with manslaughter, being convinced that he could get his client completely acquitted. He then requested a bail review, based on "new evidence" that came up in the preliminary trial. Fortunately, the accused was again refused bail. The down-to-earth judge presiding at the review saw that timing is a very subjective thing and that witnesses are usually unreliable when it comes to the duration of events.

We were satisfied that things were going to proceed as they should, with a 5-week trial beginning in November of 2014. However, we then received a call from the prosecution to attend a second meeting. This was conducted with the detective on the case present. We were told that the accused had "confessed" to his lawyer that he didn't do the shooting, that it was in fact his partner, and that he had given the partner's name to the police. The investigation would continue and, although they had the name of the alleged shooter, they had no fresh evidence to go on.

Ed and I were both very upset, as this was all based on the preliminary judge's opinion and the fact that everyone attending the crime scene was a drug addict and therefore unreliable. But somehow Rick (who was a drug addict on speed at the time of the shooting) was reliable? This stuck in my craw, and the word "deal" kept running through my head. It was obvious that the accused had decided to save his own bacon by blaming his associate as a means to a lower sentence – his cowardice raising its ugly head when he was faced with a possible sentence for second-degree murder. The lawyers on both sides had agreed to this, provided he pled guilty to manslaughter. The trial would then be concluded in one day, instead of the original five weeks that had been scheduled.

We were even further bowled over when we learned that the sentence would probably be eight years, less three years for time served (two years at time and a half), which left four years and nine months. He would also be eligible for parole after he had served two thirds of his sentence. This was the final betrayal of the legal system, completing so many years of letdown from the time Amy was about seventeen. My anger surfaced immediately.

"It's not enough!" I stated emphatically. "Eight years for a life is nothing!"

The lawyers and the detective may have agreed with me, but they know that this is the legal system in Canada today – little justice for the victims, and light sentences for criminals. We can only hope that the Harper government (the presiding federal government at the time of writing) will continue its efforts to strengthen and toughen up sentences for murderers, drunk drivers and drug dealers, who seem to be able to get away with very little prison time.

On the day of court, we listened to the "statement of fact" from the lawyers, once again claiming that the guilty man had not committed the crime, but only set it in motion. Everyone listened to our family's victim impact statements, and many tears were shed by both sides. Ed's was particularly moving, describing in detail the events of that horrible day in August of 2012, and the way that it has affected his life ever since. However, in the end, it made no difference. Although the judge had seemed to want to be stern with the young man, and told him that he hoped that he would think about what he had done every single day of his incarceration, in the end, he handed down the expected eight-year sentence.

We thanked the lawyers and the detective for all of their hard work, but reiterated that the sentence wasn't long enough. Although nothing could bring our beautiful daughter back, a harsher prison sentence might have been some vindication for the tragic loss that we had all suffered.

The guilty party seemed unremorseful, apologized glibly for his actions, and stuck his tongue out at his family when he left the courtroom. We can only hope that the great leveler, Karma, will catch up to him at some point during his life, as it so often does.

As for us, we will try to fight for tougher justice in our society, whether by joining a victims' rights group, or simply by telling people about our experiences with the legal system. As we told the reporters outside the courthouse, "The guilty man's family can visit him in prison, we can only visit our daughter in the cemetery".

Remembrance
by Fiorentina

I first met Amy when I was involved for the first time with a production with Dewdney Players, our community theatre group. It was during the cast party when in floated this amazing girl. She was dressed like a Rock Star, her blonde hair was long and wavy and she had on Jackie O dark sunglasses. I was meeting so many new people at that time and thought to myself, this girl is a celebrity of some sort, famous in some way. And if she's not, she should be and she will be, someday... I wish I didn't know now what I didn't know then; that Amy's "somedays" were limited. I quickly learned that this was the daughter of my soon-to-be dear friends, Ed and Debbie Sands. And thus began my friendship, too, with Amy. And I am so grateful for the time I did have with this incredible girl, albeit far too short, I am blessed.

I began to discover Amy was a multifaceted girl. Beautiful, witty, talented, loving and sweet. Yet she was quite troubled at times. She had her struggles. But then again, who among us has not!? This life is rarely easy and it has its share of lumps and bumps. Amy was no exception to this, no different than most of us. She just did everything in her life to the extremes!! Go Big or Go Home :)) right Amy ?!

We've all had those times when we are gazing up at the night sky and are witness to a shooting star. It is a just a mere moment in time, yet unforgettable. Amy was like a shooting star; brief, yet breathtaking, fleeting, yet so remarkable. Beautiful and brilliant, yet painstakingly, all too brief.

Amy had a heart of gold. Despite her own troubles, she loved with all her heart and soul. Even when struggling with her own issues and troubles, she would take the time for a some kind words, a loving hug , she would shed a tear, or she would dazzle you by breaking out in song or bring laughter by speaking in one of the many accents she could so flawlessly execute. She was dazzling and dynamic, yet she had inner demons that she slow danced with as well. Amy was... a BEAUTIFUL PARADOX !!

Like that shooting star, she made her impact and will not ever be forgotten! She lived more in her brief 27 years than so many do in a full lifetime!! She left behind a legacy of love that we all so intensely feel for her. Her family and friends will cherish her always. And I doubt very much, I, nor anyone, will ever encounter someone like her again. Amy was, akin to those stars, one in a million: truly unique, amazing, brilliant. Beautiful, yet far too brief.

We will forever miss you Amy.

You even make the clouds more beautiful and the heavens more spectacular !

We Love You.